As one of th…

Rely on Thomas Cook as your travelling companion on your next trip and benefit from our unique heritage.

Thomas Cook **pocket** guides

PORTO

Your travelling companion since 1873

Thomas Cook

Written and updated by Anwer Bati

Published by Thomas Cook Publishing
A division of Thomas Cook Tour Operations Limited
Company registration no. 3772199 England
The Thomas Cook Business Park, Unit 9, Coningsby Road,
Peterborough PE3 8SB, United Kingdom
Email: books@thomascook.com, Tel: +44 (0) 1733 416477
www.thomascookpublishing.com

Produced by Cambridge Publishing Management Limited
Burr Elm Court, Main Street, Caldecote CB23 7NU
www.cambridgepm.co.uk

ISBN: 978-1-84848-441-2

Series Editor: Karen Beaulah
Production/DTP: Steven Collins

Printed and bound in Spain by GraphyCems

CONTENTS

SYMBOLS KEY

The following symbols are used throughout this book:

address telephone website address email
opening times public transport connections important

The following symbols are used on the maps:

information office
airport
hospital
police station
bus station
railway station
metro
cathedral
numbers denote featured cafés & restaurants

point of interest
city
large town
small town
motorway
main road
minor road
railway
regional border

Hotels and restaurants are graded by approximate price as follows:
£ budget price ££ mid-range price £££ expensive

King Pedro IV surveys the Praça da Liberdade

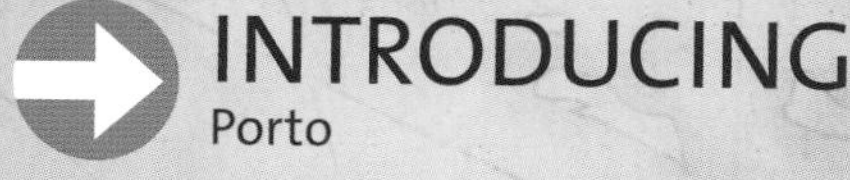

INTRODUCING
Porto

Introduction

Porto (also known as Oporto to English-speakers) is – as the name suggests – a port, and capital of the Porto district in northwest Portugal. Built on the banks of the River Douro, it is the second largest city in the country, after Lisbon, and has always been the second in economic and commercial importance. Evidence of its history is easily seen today, but the main attraction is the remarkable and fascinating old town, south of the Praça da Liberdade, designated a UNESCO World Heritage Site in 1996.

The centre of Porto is built on the granite Penaventosa Hill, sloping down to the north bank of the Douro, which is spanned by six impressive bridges. The bustling Ribeira area on the river – with its bars and restaurants – is a particular attraction, as is the city's architecture, dating from medieval times to cutting-edge modern. Porto is a lively place with several museums, a university, major performance venues and a new concert hall and opera house. The central part of the city is home to around 300,000 people, with many more in the sprawling suburbs.

One of the city's main industries is port wine – named after the city – which developed there, and for which the main market has traditionally been England, with many of the leading port houses originally owned by British firms.

Although it is a business city, Porto attracts many visitors. And its location on the Douro means that one of the most popular activities for visitors is to take a train or a cruise up the river valley, once they have explored the city itself. Visitors choose Porto for its architecture and culture (though there are relatively few formal sights), and to enjoy the city's atmosphere.

Porto grew up around the Cais da Ribeira

When to go

Porto's multifaceted charms make it a great destination all year round. The most popular time to visit is between June and September, so go in late spring or early autumn to avoid the crowds.

SEASONS & CLIMATE

For most of the year Porto enjoys a mild climate, with average summer daytime temperatures hovering around 21°C (70°F) and getting up to 25°C (77°F). The Atlantic climate means that while there is plenty of sunshine it can also rain, sometimes heavily – particularly from October to April. It's best to visit from June to September (especially July and August) if you want to avoid rain and make the most of the riverside cafés and the Douro.

ANNUAL EVENTS

There are numerous festivals, events and performances during the year. The main annual events are listed below; for further information check Ⓦ www.portoturismo.pt

February

Fantasporto Porto's main film festival, and one of the best known in Portugal – showing horror, thriller, fantasy, science fiction and cult movies. Ⓦ www.fantasporto.online.pt

April–June

Fazer a Festa A week-long theatre festival held in late April/early May, with Portuguese and international companies performing outdoors and in tents. Ⓦ www.teatroartimagem.org

Children's Week A week of theatre shows and events, in May, aimed at children.

Porto is blessed with a mild climate for most of the year

Feira do Livro (Book Fair) Going since 1920, this fair starts in mid–late May and is held for three weeks at the Rosa Mota Pavilion.
ⓐ Rua Dom Manuel II ⓣ 225 430 360 ⓦ www.feiradolivrodoporto.pt
Serralves em Festa Forty hours of exhibitions, music, dance and other free performances in Serralves park during the first weekend of June. ⓦ www.serralves.pt
Festa de São João (Feast of St John the Baptist) A couple of days of fireworks, feasts and general festivities (see page 12).

July
Jazz no Parque (Jazz in the Park) Held at Serralves park.
Encontros com o Barroco Baroque music concerts in churches.
Porto Cartoon World Festival A major cartoon event at the Museu Nacional da Imprensa, and other venues.

August
Noites Ritual Rock Rock festival, with Portuguese bands, at Palácio de Cristal.
Festas de S Bartholomeu (Feast of St Bartholomew) A colourful procession, among other celebrations.

September/October
Festival de Jazz do Porto High-quality international jazz festival held at Rivoli Teatro Municipal.
Sentidos Grátis A visual arts festival held in the streets.

December
Corrida de S Silvestre A running race, which takes place at night (when the city is decorated with Christmas lights).

Feira de Artesanato A fair promoting regional crafts, at the Palácio de Cristal. www.aarn.pt

PUBLIC HOLIDAYS

Portugal has rather a lot of public holidays, when all official buildings, many museums, most offices, and a few restaurants and bars are closed. Transport schedules are also affected. Note that 24 June is a holiday only in Porto and Braga, and not nationally.

Ano Novo (New Year's Day) 1 Jan
Entrudo/Cinzas Carnaval (Shrove Tuesday) 21 Feb 2012, 12 Feb 2013, 4 Mar 2014
Sexta-feira Santa (Good Friday) 6 Apr 2012, 29 Mar 2013, 18 Apr 2014
Dia da Liberdade (Liberation Day) 25 Apr
Dia do Trabalhador (Labour Day) 1 May
Corpo de Deus (Corpus Christi) 7 June 2012, 29 May 2013, 19 Jun 2014
Dia de Portugal (National Day of Portugal) 10 June
Festa de São João (Feast of St John the Baptist) 24 June
Assunção da Nossa Senhora (Assumption of the Virgin) 15 Aug
Implantação da República (Republic Day) 5 Oct
Todos os Santos (All Saints' Day) 1 Nov
Restauração de Independência (Independence Day) 1 Dec
Imaculada Conceição (Immaculate Conception) 8 Dec
Natal (Christmas Day) 25 Dec

Festa de São João

Although the festival celebrating the birth of St John the Baptist (patron saint of Porto) is officially on 24 June, around the time of the June solstice and the longest day of the year, the people of Porto (and the many visitors) start celebrating the night before. This is the occasion when the locals, generally famed for their reserve, really let rip.

One of the more bizarre aspects of this festival is that revellers carry plastic hammers (you'll be given one at the tourist office) with which they amiably hit one another. Restaurants and bars are packed, and festivities carry on until the morning, with fireworks being let off at midnight; the best place to watch them is Ribeira. There are also open-air music events taking place at various locations around the city, and many all-night-long parties.

On the feast day itself, things are somewhat more restrained, with church services and concerts. In the evening, the city centre has a colourful parade, Rusgas de São João, from Batalha to the Praça da Liberdade.

On the 25th, you can watch the famous, traditional and picturesque Rabelos Regatta on the Douro, starting at noon at Cabedelo. The wooden boats, *barcos rabelos*, are of the type that traditionally transported port barrels down the river. The boats are owned by the various port lodges, and bear their symbols – and some of the crews treat the competition remarkably seriously. The best place to see the race is from between the Arrábida bridge and the Dom Luís I bridge, perhaps while having lunch along the river.

Barcos rabelos, *the wooden boats on show during the Festa de São João*

History

Porto was originally founded as Cale, a Celtic trading settlement on the south bank of the Douro. It was ruled in turn by the Romans, who called it Portus Cale, the Visigoths and the Muslim Moors. Considerable conflict then followed between Muslims and Christians, and Porto – for a time capital of northern Portugal (Portucalense or Portucale – the origins of the country's name) – finally became Christian in 1092.

Three years later it became a possession of Henry of Burgundy. On the death of Ferdinand I, the last of Henry's descendants, his half-brother João (John I) founded the Portuguese royal house of Aviz. He married Philippa of Lancaster, daughter of John of Gaunt, and in 1386 Portugal and England became allies through the Treaty of Windsor.

By now Porto was a major port, and John's son Henry the Navigator, in the search for a route to the spices and other treasures of south Asia, made Portugal one of the greatest seafaring nations in the world. This laid the foundation for the Portuguese empire, with colonies such as Brazil, Mozambique, Goa and Macao. Portugal (and Porto) became increasingly prosperous, reaching the height of wealth in the 17th and 18th centuries – by now ruled by the house of Bragança – after both gold and diamonds were discovered in Brazil.

The trade in port began in 1678, and was confirmed by the Methuen Treaty between Portugal and England in 1703. The production of port is one of the city's main industries to this day.

Napoleon's armies invaded in 1807, and occupied Porto, to be driven out by British forces under General Sir Arthur Wellesley (later the Duke of Wellington) in 1809. But Portuguese prosperity took a blow: the Portuguese royal family had fled to Brazil in the face of the French threat. It returned, but relinquished Brazil as a colony.

The monarchy fell in 1910, and Portugal became a chaotically run republic until the rise of António Salazar in the 1930s. He was to rule, as dictator, until 1968 – with Portugal languishing during this period. A democratic revolution in 1974, and eventual entry to the European Community in 1986, led to the growth of economic prosperity, as well as a boom in tourism.

Following the 1996 UNESCO World Heritage listing and its nomination as European Capital of Culture in 2001, Porto underwent major development. Many buildings were restored, and its infrastructure updated – with a metro system, improved local rail links and extensions to the tram network. The Portuguese economy suffered badly, however, in the 'credit crunch' of the first decade of the 2000s, and it may be several years before the economic good times return.

Azulejos *(hand-painted tiles) adorn many historic buildings*

Lifestyle

After decades of isolation, repression and economic stagnation, the people of Portugal have adapted well to democracy and modernity, and the freedom and prosperity these have brought them. But some traditional attitudes remain, particularly among older people and those in authority. Incomes are low by Western European standards, but so are prices.

Despite its historical and economic importance, Porto's image, until recently, was quieter and less urbane than more sophisticated Lisbon, further south. Indeed, Porto has a reputation for being hard-working and somewhat conservative – the saying goes that 'Lisbon plays, Braga prays and Porto works'. But much has changed since the UNESCO and European Capital of Culture accolades, and the city now has a buzz to it and is a pretty relaxed place to visit. Hard-working northerners they may be, but the people – known for their dislike of authority – like to enjoy themselves, particularly when the weather is dry and sunny. And they like a good meal and a decent amount of drink; however, drunkenness is very rare and strongly disapproved of. The locals have a certain reserve, though they are friendly, and tend to dress fairly formally. The best dress option for a visitor is smart casual, particularly when visiting churches (there is still a strong Catholic tradition in Portugal). The Portuenses (Porto natives) are proud of their country, their city and its history, and visitors are expected to behave with decorum.

Porto has a substantial cultural life and a lively nightlife, particularly at weekends. And the biggest local passion is football, in particular FC Porto: European champions in 2004.

When Portugal hosted the Euro 2004 championships, Porto's Dragão stadium was one of the main venues.

Given the importance of the port trade, developed by British merchants, and other historical links to England, Portugal's oldest ally, British people are not only frequent visitors, but are also given a warm welcome. English is widely spoken in hotels and restaurants.

The Café Majestic, a classic Porto establishment (see page 84)

Culture

Although Porto has always been Portugal's second most important cultural centre, it has really taken off as a lively arts spot since its European Capital of Culture status in 2001. Several good museums offer art, artefacts and more unusual offerings, such as old trams. Port is also represented: you can visit the various shippers' lodges, and the Museu do Vinho do Porto.

Porto's architecture is another cultural attraction and one of the reasons why part of the city is a UNESCO World Heritage Site. This is centred on the Ribeira district (the site also covers the Mosteiro da Serra do Pilar across the Douro, and the area around Sé Cathedral), where the architecture dates from the Middle Ages to 19th-century neoclassical. Many fine churches in the centre of Porto display various architectural styles including medieval, Renaissance and Baroque, and there are important neoclassical buildings such as São Bento railway station, the Palácio da Bolsa and the Hospital Santo António. Look out for the many buildings decorated with *azulejos* (hand-painted tiles, usually with figurative designs) around the UNESCO area and the town centre. The Avenida da Boavista, and the area around it, has many impressive villas dating from the 19th century and the 1930s. Notable modern buildings in the city include the Museu de Arte Contemporânea (contemporary art museum), designed by Álvaro Siza Vieira in 1999, and Dutch architect Rem Koolhaas's Casa da Música, which opened in 2005.

Music, theatre and dance, both classical and contemporary, are very important in Porto, and there is a major orchestra, the

The Museu do Vinho do Porto tells the story of port

Orquestra Nacional do Porto. Movies too are taken seriously, with several cinemas around town (see page 31).

It's therefore well worth getting a Porto Card from a tourist office, which will give you free entry to municipal museums, unlimited use of public transport in the city, and discounts at other museums and attractions, including Douro cruises. Some shops and restaurants also offer discounts. A one-day walking card (no transport) is approximately €3.50; one day with transport around €8.50; two days €13.50; and three days €17.50. Two- and three-day cards include unlimited trips on local transport.

The six bridges (*pontes*) spanning the river aren't strictly cultural, but are well worth a mention. From east to west: Ponte do Freixo opened in 1995; Ponte São João (railway bridge; built in 1991) is now used instead of the adjacent Ponte de Dona Maria Pia bridge, dating from 1877 – designed by Gustave Eiffel. Next is the concrete Ponte do Infante (road bridge); dominating the Ribeira quayside is Ponte Dom Luís I, designed on two levels by an associate of Eiffel, and opened in 1886. Finally, near the mouth of the Douro, is Ponte da Arrábida, the largest concrete bridge in the world when it opened in 1963.

That most famous of Porto exports

MAKING THE MOST OF
Porto

Shopping

Porto is a major city, so there is no shortage of shopping, whether for local specialities or everyday items. Prices, apart from in international chains, are among the lowest you'll find in Western Europe.

The main shopping street in central Porto is Rua de Santa Catarina, where there are mainly clothes and shoe shops (shoes are cheap in Portugal), including the Via Catarina shopping centre. Also check out the Rua Passos Manuel, nearby. Several other shopping centres are dotted around the city, including two (the Peninsula and the Cidade do Porto) near the Casa da Música in the Boavista area, and the Arrábida shopping centre (with cinemas and restaurants) on the Vila Nova de Gaia side of the Douro, near the Arrábida bridge. The Boavista area also has many upmarket designer shops.

But one of the main pleasures of shopping in Porto is in finding small food, wine and craft shops. Discovering them, simply by wandering around the centre of town, is one of the highlights of any trip to Porto. Look out for old books, ceramics (including *azulejos*, Portugal's famous hand-painted tiles), textiles and jewellery.

Be sure not to forget the city's markets. The main one is the colourful semi-covered Bolhão food market, not far from Rua de Santa Catarina. The streets around it also have a number of tempting food shops, very useful for putting together a picnic. Local specialities to go for include sausages, charcuterie, cheese, pastries and salt cod. Other markets include the Feira de Antiguidades e Velharias, an antiques market at the Praça Dr Sá Carneiro on the third Saturday of each month, and the flower market, **Feira das Flores** (ⓐ Praça da Liberdade 🕒 08.00–17.00 Sun, Apr–Oct).

Wonderfully ornate delicatessen

There are several shops around town selling port and Douro wines. You can also buy port at the various lodges in Vila Nova de Gaia, and at the airport.

Some of the museums, particularly the Museu de Arte Contemporânea, also have good shops.

USEFUL SHOPPING PHRASES

What time do the shops open/close?
A que horas abrem/fecham as lojas?
A kee oras abrayng/fayshown ash lohzhash?

How much is this?
Quanto custa isto?
Kwantoo kooshta eeshtoo?

Can I try this on?
Posso experimentar este?
Possoo experimentahr aysht?

My size is ...
O meu tamanho (número) é ...
Oo mayo tamanyo (noomiroo) eh ...

I'll take this one, thank you
Levo este, obrigado
Lehvoo aysht, ohbreegahdoo

This is too large/too small/too expensive. Do you have any others?
Este é muito grande/muito pequeno/muito caro. Tem outros?
Aysht eh muingtoo grangdi/muingtoo pikaynoo/muingtoo kahroo. Tayng ohtroosh?

Eating & drinking

Portuguese cuisine can't be called sophisticated – what you will find in most restaurants amounts to versions of home or country cooking, often using fresh herbs and spices – but the food is much better than in southern Portugal and portions are extremely generous (you can ask for a *meia dose*, or half-portion). Note, however, that you will be charged for what might appear to be freebies plonked on your table, such as bread, olives and charcuterie. If you don't want them, send them back, or simply don't eat them. But eating out is relatively cheap in Portugal.

Fish and seafood are a mainstay, including the ubiquitous *bacalhau* (dried salt cod), which supposedly has enough recipes for every day of the year.

Meat is just as popular: game, beef and goat, and in particular pork: spit-roasted suckling pig is a favourite. And offal is ubiquitous on menus. Porto specialises in stewed tripe, cooked with haricot beans. Indeed the nickname for the locals is *tripeiros* ('tripe eaters'), supposedly because available meat was given to sailors, leaving only tripe to eat in the city. Portuguese menus often feature soups, including the filling bread soups, *açordas*. Brazilian dishes, and a number of Brazilian restaurants, also feature. Portuguese

PRICE CATEGORIES

The restaurant price guides given in this book indicate the approximate cost of a three-course dinner without drinks.

£ up to €15 **££** €15–50 **£££** over €50

desserts are very rich and sweet, and are often egg-based, commonly spiced with vanilla or cinnamon.

The Portuguese tend to have a very light breakfast, but a much fuller lunch and dinner. Restaurants (*restaurantes*) normally open from 12.00–15.00 and 19.00–22.00. But the lifestyle of the Portuenses is changing, and later opening hours are starting to reflect this, particularly in tourist areas. Other eateries include *toscas* – cheap family-run affairs with hearty food; *tabernas,* where you eat at a shared table; *cervejarias* serve beer and snacks; a *casa de pasto* is a dining room serving a cheap three-course meal at

Fresh fish forms the basis of the local cuisine

lunchtimes; *marisqueiras* serve fish and seafood; and *churrasqueiras* serve grilled meat.

Many restaurants include a service charge, but simpler places might not – in which case leave a 10 per cent tip. In Portugal, smoking is now banned in all places of collective public use, such as bars and restaurants, though some establishments have special permits that allow smoking in designated areas. It is always best to assume that smoking in enclosed public areas is forbidden.

You should have no difficulty finding tasty snacks, cakes, pastries and sandwiches of all kinds, including tapas, borrowed from Spain (sometimes also called *petiscos*). There are markets, of course, with cheese, charcuterie, bread, fruit and vegetables to buy – and several pleasant places to have a picnic. In winter, there are roast chestnut stalls around the city.

Portugal is one of the biggest wine producers and consumers (per head) in Europe. Portuguese wines are made with indigenous grape varieties, and are of a high standard, particularly those designated DOC, although house wines (*vinho da casa*) are good value and perfectly drinkable. Local Douro wines, such as white Planalto, are very pleasing. Vinho Verde is young, very dry and slightly fizzy – both whites and (normally weaker) reds.

The best-known wine from the area though is port, which includes: Ruby (young and fruity, and the cheapest), Tawny (aged in wood), Vintage (aged for years in bottles and the most expensive), Colheita (Tawny from a single year) and white port, normally drunk as an aperitif. Madeira is a fortified wine from the Portuguese-ruled Atlantic island of the same name. The best-known Portuguese spirit is *aguardente* – made from different fruits.

USEFUL DINING PHRASES

I would like a table for ... people
Queria uma mesa para ... pessoas
Kireea ooma mehza para ... pesoash

May I have the bill, please?
Pode dar-me a conta, por favor?
Pohd dahr-muh er kohngta, poor favohr?

Waiter/waitress!
Faz favor!
Fash favohr!

Could I have it well cooked/medium/rare, please?
Posso escolher bem passado/médio/mal passado, por favor?
Possoo ishkoolyer bayng pasahdoo/maydioo/mahl pasahdoo, poor favohr?

I am a vegetarian. Does this contain meat?
Sou vegetariano. Isto tem carne?
Soh vezhetahreeahnoo. Ishtoo tehng kahrni?

Where is the toilet (restroom) please?
Por favor, onde são os lavabos?
Poor favohr, ohngdee sowng oos lavahboosh?

I would like a cup of/two cups of/another coffee/tea
Queria uma chávena de/duas chávenas de/outro café/chá
Kireea ooma shahvna di/dooash shahvnash di/ohtroo kafeh/shah

Entertainment & nightlife

Porto has a lively nightlife, particularly at weekends in summer. For a start, many of the main sights, such as the cathedral, the Dom Luís I bridge and the Clérigos Tower, are illuminated at night, so simply walking around is something to look forward to.

Plenty of bars and cafés allow for a late drink after dinner – in good weather you can sit outside on Ribeira quay or at the mouth of the Douro and enjoy the river view – and a decent selection of clubs and discos around town delay bedtime. The Foz do Douro area is the most happening place to head for in summer, particularly the Avenida do Brasil. And the last five or six years have seen a range of new bars and restaurants, many glass-fronted and with roof terraces, opening up on the quayside at Vila Nova de Gaia.

Theatre performances are in Portuguese, of course, but there are also many musical and dance performances to go to, where language isn't a barrier. Major international artists sometimes perform at venues such as the Teatro Nacional de São João, the Rivoli Teatro Municipal, the Coliseu do Porto and the Casa da Música.

There are also several music festivals during the year, including the Jazz Festival (centred on the Rivoli theatre), the outdoor Jazz no Parque on the old tennis court of Serralves park and Noites do Palácio and Noites Ritual Rock, both at the Palácio de Cristal. Major rock performances are most likely to be at the **Coliseu** (ⓐ Rua de Passos Manuel 137 ⓣ 223 394 940 ⓦ www.coliseudoporto.pt Ⓜ Metro: D to S Bento or A, B, C, E to Bolhão), dating from the 1940s, which also stages opera and other spectacles.

There is no shortage of swanky bars in Porto

If you want to catch a movie, there are a number of cinemas in central Porto, mostly showing films in their original language – including English – with Portuguese subtitles. In particular the **Cinema Batalha** (ⓐ Praça da Batalha 47 ⓣ 222 011 913 Metro: D to S Bento), opened in 1947, has two bars and a terrace (until 02.00 during the week, and 04.00 at weekends) as well as a restaurant (12.00–15.00, 20.00–22.30) and a coffee shop.

There is a **multiscreen cinema** (ⓐ Centro Commerical Cidade do Porto, Rua Gonçalo Sampaio 350 ⓣ 226 009 164 Metro: A, B, C, E to Casa da Música) in the Cidade do Porto shopping centre in Boavista.

You will find events listings in the free monthly *cultura.norte*, and the quarterly *Agenda do Porto* (in Portuguese and English ⓦ www.cm-porto.pt): both available from tourist offices and hotels; and on the local tourist website ⓦ www.portoturismo.pt

Sport & relaxation

SPECTATOR SPORTS

Football

You can share the local obsession with football by watching **FC Porto** (ⓐ Estádio do Dragão ⓣ 225 570 400 ⓦ www.fcporto.pt (in Portuguese and English) ⓜ Metro: A, B, C, E to Estádio do Dragão) or Porto's less well-known football club, **Boavista FC** (ⓐ Estádio do Bessa, Rua 1° de Janeiro ⓣ 226 071 004/5 ⓦ www.boavistafc.pt ⓜ Metro: A, B, C, E to Casa da Música).

PARTICIPATION SPORTS

Vigorous and challenging activities, including riding, can be booked through **Arrepio-Animação** (ⓐ Rua Prof Antão Almeida Garret 229 ⓣ 228 303 940). Tennis courts include **Lawn Tennis Clube da Foz** (ⓐ Rua João Martins Branco 154 ⓣ 226 180 933) and **Oporto Cricket and Lawn Tennis Club** (ⓐ Rua do Campo Alegre 532 ⓣ 226 091 719). To find a gym, consult the tourist office website (ⓦ www.portoturismo.pt) or your nearest tourist office.

Golf

Quinta da Barca, 30 km (19 miles) from Porto. ⓐ Barca do Lago ⓣ 253 969 060 ⓦ www.golfebarca.com.

Estela, 35 km (22 miles) away. ⓐ Rio Alto ⓣ 252 601 567/814 ⓦ www.estelagolf.pt

Watersports

Don't swim in the sea anywhere near the centre of Porto. Go to the **Clube Fluvial Portuense** instead (ⓐ Rua Aleixo Mota

226 198 460 clubefluvialportuense@clix.pt 08.00–22.00 Mon–Fri, 09.00–18.00 Sat, 09.00–13.00 Sun (summer); 08.00–21.00 Mon–Fri, 09.00–18.00 Sat, 09.00–13.00 Sun (winter) Bus: 207 to Pasteleira).

There's no better way to see the city than a cruise down the Douro

You can learn to surf at **Surfing Life Clube Matosinhos** (ⓐ Praça Cidade S Salvador 295 ⓣ 93 756 7092 ⓦ www.surfinglifeclub.com) or **Escola de Surf do Norte** (ⓐ Praia de Matosinhos ⓣ 229 379 665/963 156 441 ⓦ www.clubedesportoaventura.web.pt).

BOAT & BUS TRIPS

There are all sorts of boat trips along the Douro, in either simple *rabelos* or more lavish craft, many with English-speaking guides. The best central point of information and to book is **Porto Tours** (by the cathedral) (ⓐ Torre Medieval, Calçada D Pedro Pitões 15 ⓣ 222 000 073 ⓦ www.portotours.com), where you can also book bus tours both in or out of the city. For hop-on, hop-off open-top double-decker guided bus tours of the city, call ⓣ 808 200 166.

Accommodation

Porto has all types of accommodation, though much of it is outside the UNESCO World Heritage area. Note that central hotel accommodation is in short supply during the city's many business events and in summer; however, outside summer, it is often easier to get a room at weekends than during the week. Always make sure you book well in advance.

Unless you have booked an inclusive package, it pays to investigate thoroughly on the web. The Porto tourist website (W www.portoturismo.pt) carries a comprehensive list of hotels and their facilities, and provides links to the hotels' own websites. The recommendations below are only a few of the good hotels to choose from. The ratings indicate the average price per double room per night. Some rooms, particularly those with views, may be more expensive than the ratings suggest, others might be cheaper. Many hotels include a buffet breakfast in their rates, others charge a supplement.

Although you might want to stay in or near the UNESCO area for easy access to the main sights, don't automatically dismiss the Foz and Boavista areas, which are attractive alternatives and boast some of the best hotels in Porto.

PRICE CATEGORIES

The approximate cost of a double room, usually including breakfast, is rated as follows:

£ up to €100 **££** €100–150 **£££** over €150

HOTELS

Hotel Boa Vista £ A late-19th-century hotel at the mouth of the Douro, with modernised rooms (the most expensive with a sea view) and a rooftop swimming pool. Not far from Serralves park. ⓐ Esplanada do Castelo 58 (West of the city centre) ⓣ 225 320 020 ⓦ www.hotelboavista.com Bus: 200 to Mercado da Foz

Hotel São José £ Small, family-run traditional hotel near the World Heritage area. ⓐ Rua da Alegria 172 (The city centre) ⓣ 222 080 261 ⓦ www.saojosehotelporto.com Metro: A, B, C, E to Bolhão

Residencial dos Aliados £ A good, simple, central budget choice in an Art Nouveau building. Some rooms can be noisy. ⓐ Rua Eliseo de Melo 27 (The city centre) ⓣ 222 004 853 ⓦ www.residencialaliados.com Metro: D to Aliados

Eurostars Hotel das Artes £–££ Very good value 4-star hotel, just by the Museu Soares dos Reis, and close to the Palácio de Cristal. A good location for most of Porto's sights. ⓐ Rua do Rosário 160–164 (The city centre) ⓣ 222 071 250 ⓦ www.eurostarsdasartes.com Bus: 3, 6, 20, 24, 35, 37, 52, 78

Hotel da Bolsa £–££ Close to the old stock exchange building, convenient for exploring the Ribeira area. Built on the site of an old monastery, it has an impressive 19th-century façade; the rooms, however, are functional and modern, with the best having a view of the river. ⓐ Rua Ferreira Borges 101 (The World Heritage area & Vila Nova de Gaia) ⓣ 222 026 768 ⓦ www.hoteldabolsa.com Metro: D to S Bento

Grande Hotel do Porto ££ Porto's oldest existing hotel, dating from 1880, is situated right in the heart of the main shopping area. The rooms, last refurbished in 2002, are modern, but the public areas, including the good restaurant, retain their period charm. ⓐ Rua de Santa Catarina 197 (The city centre) ⓣ 222 076 690 ⓦ www.grandehotelporto.com Metro: A, B, C, E to Bolhão

Hotel Fénix Porto ££ A modern hotel, officially 4-star, but with reasonable prices. Situated near the Rotunda de Boavista, and the Casa da Música. ⓐ Rua Gonçalo Sampaio 282 (West of the city centre) ⓣ 226 071 800 ⓦ www.hfhotels.com Metro: A, B, C, E to Casa da Música

Mercure Porto Centro ££ Very well placed for both the city centre and Ribeira, this comfortable hotel by Porto's main theatre is a good choice. ⓐ Praça da Batalha 116 (The city centre) ⓣ 222 043 300 ⓦ www.mercure.com Metro: D to S Bento

Hotel Dom Henrique ££–£££ Basically a business hotel, but with good rooms and facilities, and great views from the bar on the 17th floor. A convenient location for central Porto. ⓐ Rua Guedes Azevado 179 (The city centre) ⓣ 223 401 616 ⓦ www.hoteldomhenrique.pt Metro: A, B, C, D, E Trindade

Pestana Porto ££–£££ On the Douro in the Ribeira area with fine views of the river from the best of the well-appointed rooms. ⓐ Praça da Ribeira 1 (The World Heritage area & Vila Nova de Gaia) ⓣ 223 402 300 ⓦ www.pestana.com Metro: D to S Bento (then a 15-minute walk)

Infante de Sagres £££ Porto's most famous hotel is full of charm and character, with plush public areas furnished with antiques, a stairwell with stained glass, and an old-fashioned lift. There is a restaurant, a bar, a spa room and a courtyard where you can have a drink or take breakfast if the weather's good. Rooms are

Traditional luxury at the Infante de Sagres

extremely comfortable. Very well located for the UNESCO area. ⓐ Praça Filipa de Lencastre 62 (The World Heritage area & Vila Nova de Gaia) ⓣ 223 398 500 ⓦ www.hotelinfantesagres.pt ⓥ Metro: D to Aliados

Sheraton Porto Hotel & Spa £££ This glitzy luxury hotel, on 12 floors – with a spa and pool – has state-of-the-art rooms offering considerable comfort. Its location in Boavista means prices are lower than in some less good central hotels. The buffet breakfast is excellent. ⓐ Rua do Tenente Valadim 146 (West of the city centre) ⓣ 220 404 000 ⓦ www.sheraton.com/porto ⓥ Metro: A, B, C, E to Francos

The Yeatman £££ Opened in late 2010, this is set to become the city's most fashionable hotel. Its hillside location affords great views of the Douro and Ribeira quay, the rooms are spacious, with terraces, and there is a pool and a spa. The hotel is particularly aimed at port and wine lovers – not least because it is owned by the company behind Taylor's. ⓐ Rua do Choupelo (The World Heritage area & Vila Nova de Gaia) ⓣ 220 133 100 ⓦ www.theyeatman.com ⓥ Metro: D to General Torres

YOUTH HOSTELS

Pousada da Juventude do Porto £ Porto's excellent youth hostel has a view of the mouth of the Douro, a bar, a kitchen, Internet access and parking. There are several types of accommodation, but make sure you book in advance. ⓐ Rua Paulo da Gama 551 (West of the city centre) ⓣ 226 177 257 ⓦ www.movijovem.pt, www.pousadasjuventude.pt ⓥ Bus: 207 to Pasteleira

THE BEST OF PORTO

Porto doesn't have a huge number of formal sights or attractions, and those it does have are mainly within walking distance of each other or a short metro or taxi ride away. You'll get as much from relaxing and enjoying the lifestyle and atmosphere as you will from trying to pack in as much as possible.

TOP 10 ATTRACTIONS

- **Cais da Ribeira (Ribeira Quay)** The quayside is a pleasure to walk along and is where you will find some of the town's liveliest bars and restaurants (see page 59).

- **Torre dos Clérigos (Clérigos Tower)** Climbing up the tower will reward you with incomparable views of the town centre and the World Heritage area (see page 63).

- **Fundação de Serralves Museu de Arte Contemporânea (Serralves Foundation Museum of Contemporary Art)** A few hours spent at the museum and in the park will be one of the highlights of your trip (see page 92).

- **Sé Catedral** Porto's most important building, and a major landmark (see page 67).

- **Palácio da Bolsa (Stock Exchange Palace)** A guided tour around the grand interior of the neoclassical former stock exchange is well worthwhile (see page 64).

- **Igreja de São Francisco (Church of St Francis)** In a city full of impressive churches, the rococo interior of this one is perhaps the most outstanding (see page 63).

- **Festa de São João (Feast of St John the Baptist)** If you're in town during the festival (24 June), you'll see the Portuenses at their most lively (see page 12).

- **Visit to a port lodge** It would be a shame to visit Porto without heading to one of the port lodges for a tasting (see page 66).

- **A walk along one of the Douro bridges** Walking along any of the central bridges will give you superb views (see page 20).

- **A cruise down the Douro Valley** Cruises can be as short as an hour or much, much longer. A train ride up the valley is equally picturesque (see page 34).

Ornate windows typical of Ribeira

Suggested itineraries

HALF-DAY: PORTO IN A HURRY

You'll have time to see just the World Heritage area, including a visit to the Clérigos Tower, the cathedral and the Ribeira district.

1 DAY: TIME TO SEE A LITTLE MORE

Now you can also walk across the Dom Luís I bridge to visit the Mosteiro da Serra, see more of central Porto and have time to pop into a museum, such as the Museu Nacional Soares dos Reis, or a church or two. You might also have time for some shopping in the Rua de Santa Catarina.

2–3 DAYS: TIME TO SEE MUCH MORE

Now you can really get to know Porto. You shouldn't miss the Museu de Arte Contemporânea and Serralves park, and go to the nearby Boavista area to see the villas of the wealthy and the Casa da Música. You should also have time to visit the Museu do Carro Eléctrico (Tram Museum), and the nearby Palácio Cristal park, the Museu Romântico and maybe the Museu do Vinho do Porto. Also visit the Palácio da Bolsa and the neighbouring Casa do Infante. If you can, also try to visit the Gaia district and its port lodges.

LONGER: ENJOYING PORTO TO THE FULL

If you're in Porto for longer, you can really relax, enjoy a few long lunches, see a bit of the newer parts of the city, visit the Foz area and the mouth of the Douro, and perhaps take a cruise or boat trip up the the Douro Valley or visit attractive towns (around an hour away) such as Guimarães and Braga.

Don't miss the medieval streets of the World Heritage area

Something for nothing

Walking around is the cheapest and one of the most rewarding things you can do in Porto. You'll mostly be walking anyway, around the city centre and Ribeira, but you should also cross the Dom Luís I bridge to Vila Nova de Gaia, where most of the port lodges, such as Graham's, are free to visit. You can also walk along the Douro to the mouth of the river and the attractive seaside quarter. Boavista is another appealing area to visit, stretching from the centre of town to the sea along the Avenida da Boavista. Make sure you stop to admire the Casa da Música.

Porto's many churches, including the cathedral, are also free, as are parks such as the Palácio Cristal, the Parque da Cidade and many other green spaces around town. Some museums and sights, such as Casa Tait, are also free; others, such as the Museu Romântico, are free at weekends; and the Soares dos Reis museum is free on Sunday mornings and public holidays. And, although Porto is cheaper than most European cities, window shopping or a visit to the Bolhão, one of the other markets or a tempting food shop needn't cost a penny.

Then there are Porto's main festivals, many of which, such as **Serralves em Festa** (08.00 Sat–24.00 Sun www.serralves.pt) during the first weekend of June, offer free events. And taking part in the exuberant Festa de São João (see page 12) doesn't have to cost you anything extra. Visiting the Porto Book Fair in June (see page 10) is also free.

If you buy a Porto Card (see page 20), of course, all the municipal museums and local public transport are free, plus you'll get substantial discounts at other attractions.

The sublime exterior of the São Nicolau Church – free to all

When it rains

It can rain rather a lot in Porto, particularly in winter, and showers can be pretty persistent. But that shouldn't stop you from enjoying yourself, although walking on the cobbled streets of the old city or on the slippery pavements of the city centre, can be rather hazardous – make sure you take suitable shoes.

The metro system is, however, clean, modern and efficient, so it's a good option for getting around, as are the reasonably priced taxis which you will find at ranks around town. So you can stay dry when making your way to one of the city's smaller museums or to one of Porto's churches, which you might not have thought of going to on a sunny day. A ride in one of Porto's ancient trams is a fun option. And a warming port tasting at one of the shippers' lodges, as well as a tour, might be just the thing to go for.

Otherwise, the most enjoyable way to escape the rain is to pop into a café for a drink or to a restaurant to treat yourself to a lengthy lunch, maybe trying out some of the more unusual local specialities. Most restaurants on the Ribeira quayside have umbrellas outside, so there's no need to hide indoors. And some of the cafés along both sides of the Douro are glass-fronted, so you can still enjoy a view of the river. Porto also has several shopping centres, most with cafés, so you could always do a bit of shopping while you wait for the rain to subside.

Since most films shown in Portugal are in their original language, with subtitles, you should easily be able to find an English-language film to watch if you really can't face the rain.

Porto's antiquated trams are a great way to see the city – whatever the weather

On arrival

TIME DIFFERENCE

Portugal follows Greenwich Mean Time (GMT): from the end of March to the end of October, the clocks are put ahead one hour.

ARRIVING

By air

Francisco Sá Carneiro airport is 15 km (9 miles) northwest of Porto's city centre. Note that, although the airport is state-of-the-art, you might have to walk some distance to get to the baggage hall. Arrivals are on the ground floor: café, newsagent and ATM machine to the left, car-hire firms to the right; with a state tourist office in the concourse.

Checking in at Francisco Sá Carneiro airport

It takes around 30–35 minutes to get into central Porto by car or taxi. The metro (line E) takes about the same time and runs every 25 minutes.

Aeroporto Francisco Sá Carneiro t 229 432 400
w www.ana-aeroportos.pt

By rail

Long-distance trains arrive at Campanhã station to the east of Porto. Take a metro or taxi to your hotel or get a local train to São Bento railway station in the city centre (about ten minutes) and then take a metro or taxi.

Campanhã a Largo da Estação de Campanhã 05.00–01.45
São Bento a Praça Almeida Garrett 06.15–20.15
CP (Comboios de Portugal/Portuguese Railways) t 808 208 208
w www.cp.pt

By road

If coming from the north, you are likely to be arriving on the IC1 or the A3/IP1; for the city centre, follow signs to Aliados or Centro – the city centre can get very congested and beware the complex one-way systems. Car parks include: a Rua Fernandes Tomás, a Avenida da Boavista, a Rua de Cervantes and a Rua de Cedofeita.

FINDING YOUR FEET

The pace of life in Porto isn't very different to back home. With the help of a map you should have no difficulty in finding your way around; everything is well signposted, and many locals speak at least a little English and will be helpful.

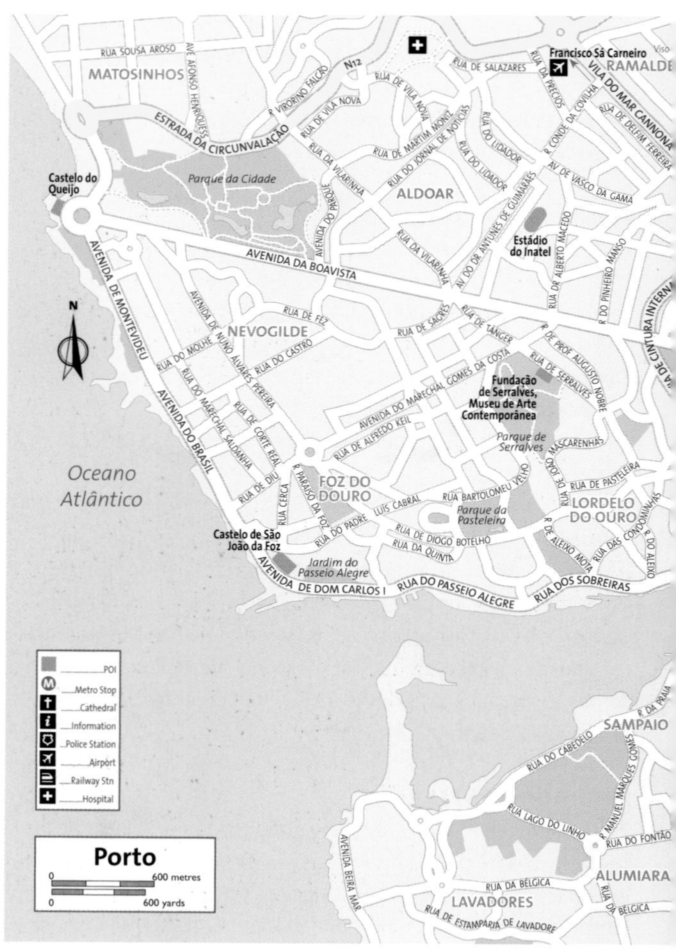

RUA SOUSA AROSO
MATOSINHOS
AVE AFONSO HENRIQUES
R VIRORINO FALCÃO
N12
RUA DE VILA NOVA
RUA DE SALAZARES
RUA DA PRECIOS
Francisco Sá Carneiro
RAMALDE
VILA DO MAR CANNONA
RUA DE DELFIM FERREIRA
R CONDE DA COVILHA
ESTRADA DA CIRCUNVALAÇÃO
RUA DE VILA NOVA
RUA DA VILARINHA
RUA DE MARTIM MONIZ
RUA DO JORNAL DE NOTICIAS
RUA DO LIDADOR
RUA DO LIDADOR
AV DE VASCO DA GAMA
Castelo do Queijo
Parque da Cidade
AVENIDA DO PARQUE
ALDOAR
AV DO DR ANTUNES DE GUIMARÃES
RUA DR ALBERTO MACEDO
Estádio do Inatel
R DO PINHEIRO MANSO
AVENIDA DA BOAVISTA
RUA DA VILARINHA
AVENIDA DE MONTEVIDEU
N
AVENIDA DE NUNO ÁLVARES PEREIRA
RUA DE FEZ
NEVOGILDE
RUA DE SAGRES
RUA DE TANGER
R DE PROF AUGUSTO NOBRE
RUA DE SERRALVES
RUA DO MOLHE
RUA DO CASTRO
AVENIDA DO MARECHAL GOMES DA COSTA
Fundação de Serralves, Museu de Arte Contemporânea
RUA DO MARECHAL SALDANHA
RUA DE CORTE REAL
AVENIDA DE ALFREDO KEIL
RUA DE ALFREDO KEIL
AVENIDA DO BRASIL
Parque de Serralves
RUA DE JOÃO MASCARENHAS
Oceano Atlântico
RUA DE DIU
R PARAÍSO DA FOZ
FOZ DO DOURO
RUA CERCA
LUÍS CABRAL
RUA BARTOLOMEU VELHO
RUA DE PASTELEIRA
LORDELO DO OURO
Parque da Pasteleira
RUA DAS CONDOMINHAS
R DO ALEIXO
Castelo de São João da Foz
RUA DO PADRE
RUA DE DIOGO BOTELHO
RUA DA QUINTA
R DE ALEIXO MOTA
Jardim do Passeio Alegre
AVENIDA DE DOM CARLOS I
RUA DO PASSEIO ALEGRE
RUA DOS SOBREIRAS
POI
Metro Stop
Cathedral
Information
Police Station
Airport
Railway Stn
Hospital
R DA PRAIA
SAMPAIO
RUA DO CABEDELO
R MANUEL MARQUES GOMES
RUA LAGO DO LINHO
RUA DO FONTÃO
AVENIDA BEIRA MAR
ALUMIARA
RUA DA BÉLGICA
LAVADORES
RUA DA BÉLGICA
RUA DE ESTAMPARIA DE LAVADORE
Porto
0
600 metres
0
600 yards

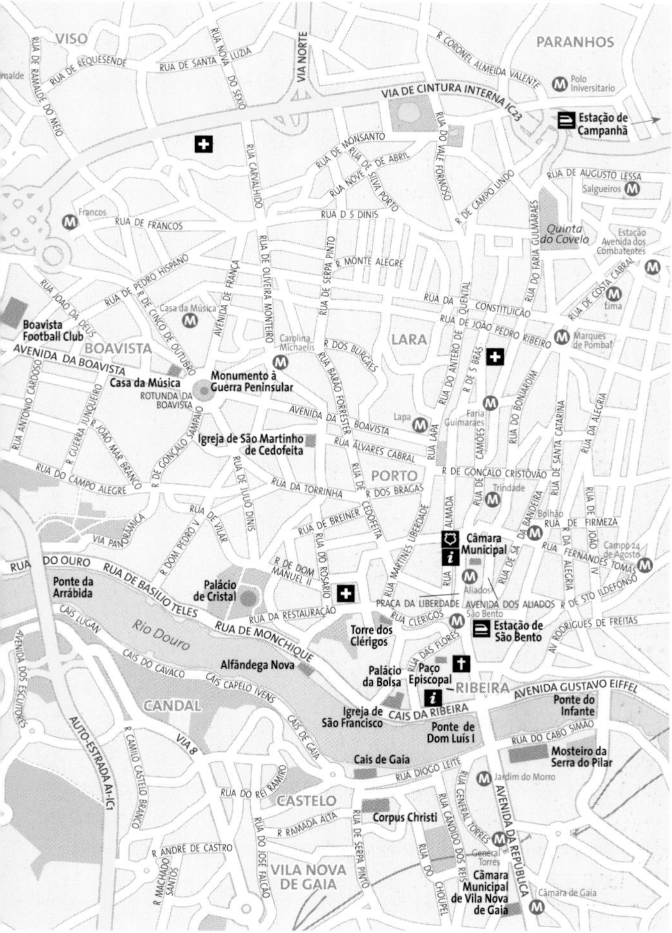

VISO
PARANHOS
RUA DE RAMALDE DO MEIO
RUA DE REQUESENDE
RUA DE SANTA LUZIA
RUA NOVA DO SEXIO
VIA NORTE
R CORONEL ALMEIDA VALENTE
Polo Universitario
VIA DE CINTURA INTERNA IC23
Estação de Campanhã
RUA CARVALHIDO
RUA DE MONSANTO
RUA NOVE DE ABRIL
RUA DE SILVA PORTO
RUA DO VALE FORMOSO
R DE CAMPO LINDO
RUA DE AUGUSTO LESSA
Salgueiros
Francos
RUA DE FRANCOS
RUA D S DINIS
Quinta do Covelo
Estação Avenida dos Combatentes
RUA DO FARIA GUIMARÃES
RUA DE OLIVEIRA MONTEIRO
RUA DE SERPA PINTO
R MONTE ALEGRE
RUA DE COSTA CABRAL
RUA DE PEDRO HISPANO
R DE CINCO DE OUTUBRO
AVENIDA DE FRANÇA
Casa da Música
RUA JOÃO DA DEUS
RUA DA CONSTITUIÇÃO
RUA DE JOÃO PEDRO RIBEIRO
Marques de Pombal
Boavista Football Club
BOAVISTA
AVENIDA DA BOAVISTA
Carolina Michaelis
R DOS BURGÃES
LARA
RUA DO ANTERO DE QUENTAL
R DE S BRAS
Casa da Música
Monumento à Guerra Peninsular
ROTUNDA DA BOAVISTA
RUA ANTONIO CARDOSO
R GUERRA JUNQUEIRO
R JOÃO MAR BRANCO
RUA DE GONÇALO SAMPAIO
AVENIDA DA BOAVISTA
RUA BARÃO FORRESTER
Lapa
RUA LAPA
Faria Guimarães
RUA DO BONJARDIM
RUA DE SANTA CATARINA
RUA DA ALEGRIA
Igreja de São Martinho de Cedofeita
RUA ÁLVARES CABRAL
RUA DO CAMPO ALEGRE
RUA DE JULIO DINIS
RUA DA TORRINHA
PORTO
R DE GONÇALO CRISTÓVÃO
Trindade
R DOS BRAGAS
RUA DE CEDOFEITA
RUA DE VILAR
RUA DE BREINER
RUA MARTINES LIBERDADE
RUA ALMADA
RUA DA BANDEIRA
Bolhão
RUA DE FIRMEZA
VIA PANORÂMICA
RUA DOM PEDRO V
RUA DO ROSÁRIO
Câmara Municipal
RUA DE SÁ
RUA FERNANDES TOMÁS
Campo 24 de Agosto
RUA DO OURO
Ponte da Arrábida
RUA DE BASILIO TELES
Palácio de Cristal
R DE DOM MANUEL II
Aliados
PRAÇA DA LIBERDADE
AVENIDA DOS ALIADOS
R DE STO ILDEFONSO
CAIS LUGAN
Rio Douro
RUA DA RESTAURAÇÃO
RUA CLÉRIGOS
São Bento
Estação de São Bento
AV RODRIGUES DE FREITAS
AVENIDA DOS ESCULTORES
RUA DE MONCHIQUE
Torre dos Clérigos
RUA DAS FLORES
CAIS DO CAVACO
Alfândega Nova
Palácio da Bolsa
Paço Episcopal
RIBEIRA
AVENIDA GUSTAVO EIFFEL
CAIS CAPELO IVENS
CANDAL
Igreja de São Francisco
CAIS DA RIBEIRA
Ponte do Infante
AUTO-ESTRADA A1-IC1
VIA 8
CAIS DE GAIA
Ponte de Dom Luís I
RUA DO CABO SIMÃO
Mosteiro da Serra do Pilar
R CAMILO CASTELO BRANCO
Cais de Gaia
RUA DIOGO LEITE
Jardim do Morro
RUA DO REI RAMIRO
CASTELO
RUA GENERAL TORRES
AVENIDA DA REPÚBLICA
Corpus Christi
RUA CANDIDO DOS REIS
R RAMADA ALTA
RUA DO JOSÉ FALCÃO
RUA DE SERPA PINTO
RUA DO CHOUPEL
General Torres
R ANDRÉ DE CASTRO
R MACHADO SANTOS
VILA NOVA DE GAIA
Câmara Municipal de Vila Nova de Gaia
Câmara de Gaia

Comfortable shoes with non-slip soles are a good idea, to cope with steep cobbled streets and slippery pavements when it rains.

Portuguese can be difficult for foreigners to pronounce. A good idea is to write down your destination, to give to a taxi driver or ticket office, for example.

ORIENTATION

The heart of the city centre is Praça da Liberdade and the Avenida dos Aliados, dominated at the northern end by the Câmara Municipal (Town Hall), which is beautifully illuminated at night. The Boavista area and Serralves park are both some way to the west. To the south you'll find the old town, the Ribeira area and the Douro. Across the river from Ribeira is Vila Nova de Gaia. The cathedral and the neighbouring Paço Episcopal (bishop's palace) are key landmarks to orient yourself – as is the Torre dos Clérigos (Clérigos Tower), which can be seen from much of the city. S Bento station, just south of Praça da Liberdade is another helpful landmark, as is the Douro, which, wherever you are, will almost certainly be downhill.

GETTING AROUND

Porto is well served by public transport, although many of the sights are within walking distance of one another. The best way to get round is by metro (🕒 06.00–01.00 daily), which is clean, comfortable and efficient; the stations are rather discreetly marked. The extensive bus system (🕒 06.00–21.00 daily) also has a network of night buses. (Bus numbers may change as Porto's transport system develops.) Bus and metro ticket prices are modest. You can buy metro tickets from machines at the stops,

IF YOU GET LOST, TRY ...

Excuse me, do you speak English?
Desculpe, fala inglês?
Dishkoolper, fahla eenglaysh?

Excuse me, is this the right way to ... the cathedral/ the tourist office/the castle/the old town?
Desculpe, é este o caminho certo para ... a catedral/ os serviços de informações turísticas (o turismo)/ o castelo/a cidade velha?
Dishkoolper, eh aysht oo kameenyo sehrtoo para ... er katidrahl/ oos sirveessoos de eemfoormasoyesh tooreehshteekash (oo tooreesmoo)/oo kastehloo/er seedahd vehlya?

Can you point to it on my map?
Pode indicá-lo no meu mapa?
Pohd eendeecahloo noo mayo mahpa?

and bus tickets on board or at the STCP bus company's offices and at tobacconists. They are cheaper if you buy them in advance. Don't forget to validate your ticket when you board a bus, by inserting it in the machine by the driver.

The Andante 24 pass (around €3.35) allows unlimited use of public transport for 24 hours after the first validation. The Porto Card (see page 20) also includes unlimited use of transport. All passes must be validated.

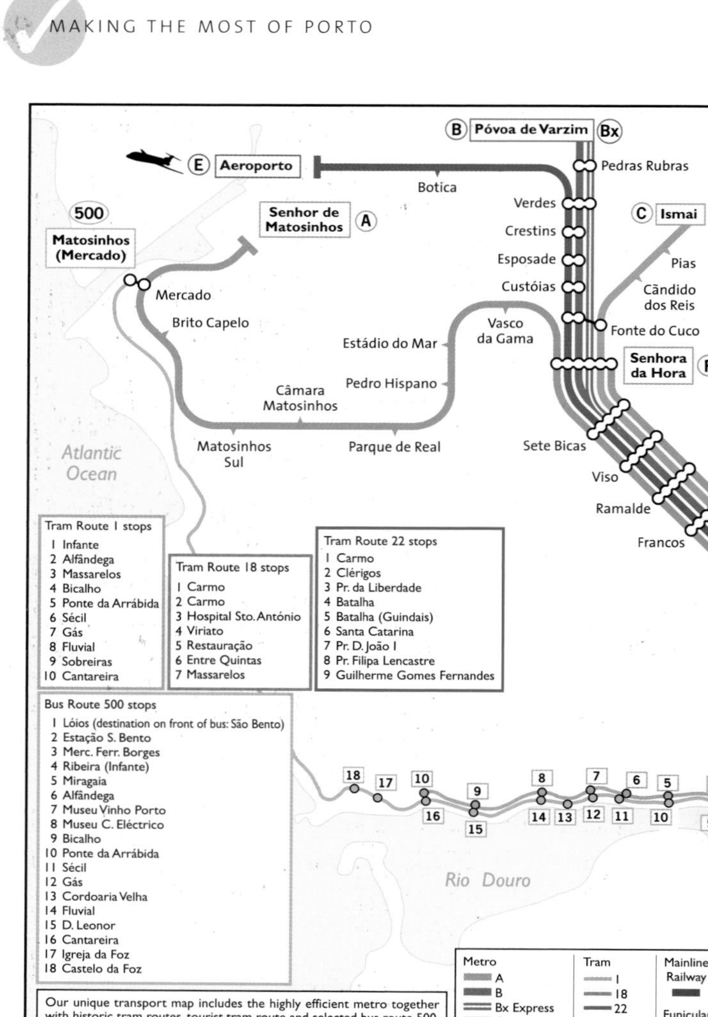

B
Póvoa de Varzim
Bx
E
Aeroporto
Pedras Rubras
Botica
Verdes
500
Senhor de Matosinhos
A
C
Ismai
Matosinhos (Mercado)
Crestins
Esposade
Pias
Custóias
Cândido dos Reis
Mercado
Brito Capelo
Vasco da Gama
Fonte do Cuco
Estádio do Mar
Senhora da Hora
F
Pedro Hispano
Câmara Matosinhos
Matosinhos Sul
Parque de Real
Sete Bicas
Atlantic Ocean
Viso
Ramalde
Francos
Tram Route 1 stops
1 Infante
2 Alfândega
3 Massarelos
4 Bicalho
5 Ponte da Arrábida
6 Sécil
7 Gás
8 Fluvial
9 Sobreiras
10 Cantareira
Tram Route 18 stops
1 Carmo
2 Carmo
3 Hospital Sto. António
4 Viriato
5 Restauração
6 Entre Quintas
7 Massarelos
Tram Route 22 stops
1 Carmo
2 Clérigos
3 Pr. da Liberdade
4 Batalha
5 Batalha (Guindais)
6 Santa Catarina
7 Pr. D. João I
8 Pr. Filipa Lencastre
9 Guilherme Gomes Fernandes
Bus Route 500 stops
1 Lóios (destination on front of bus: São Bento)
2 Estação S. Bento
3 Merc. Ferr. Borges
4 Ribeira (Infante)
5 Miragaia
6 Alfândega
7 Museu Vinho Porto
8 Museu C. Eléctrico
9 Bicalho
10 Ponte da Arrábida
11 Sécil
12 Gás
13 Cordoaria Velha
14 Fluvial
15 D. Leonor
16 Cantareira
17 Igreja da Foz
18 Castelo da Foz
18
17
10
9
8
7
6
5
16
15
14
13
12
11
10
Rio Douro
Our unique transport map includes the highly efficient metro together with historic tram routes, tourist tram route and selected bus route 500. We have included bus route 500 since this will take you directly from the city centre to the Port Wine Museum. Not only that but it is a pleasant route out to the Atlantic coast which makes for a refreshing interlude from city life. Several interesting bars, cafés and restaurants are yours to explore on the way. Even a heli-pad at stop number 8 awaits the daring among you!
Metro
A
B
Bx Express
C
D
E
F
Tram
1
18
22
Mainline Railway
Funicular
Bus
Bus, Tram & Funicular stops

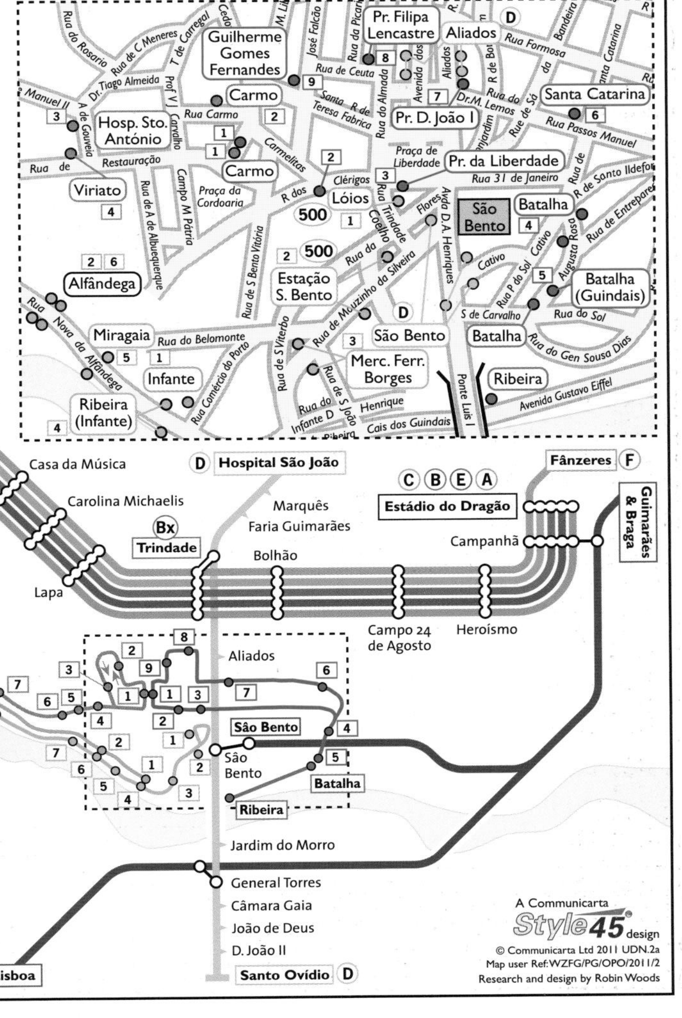

Pr. Filipa Lencastre
Aliados
Guilherme Gomes Fernandes
Carmo
Santa Catarina
Hosp. Sto. António
Pr. D. João I
Pr. da Liberdade
Viriato
Lóios
São Bento
Batalha
Alfândega
Estação S. Bento
Batalha (Guindais)
Miragaia
São Bento
Batalha
Merc. Ferr. Borges
Infante
Ribeira
Ribeira (Infante)
Rua Formosa
Rua de Ceuta
Rua Carmo
Rua de Restauração
Praça da Cordoaria
Rua 31 de Janeiro
Rua Passos Manuel
Rua do Belomonte
Rua de Mouzinho da Silveira
Avda D.A. Henriques
Ponte Luís I
Avenida Gustavo Eiffel
Cais dos Guindais
Rua do Sol
Rua do Gen Sousa Dias
Rua Nova da Alfândega
Rua Comércio do Porto
Rua de S Bento Vitória
Rua de S Viterbo
Rua do Infante D Henrique
Praça de Liberdade
Casa da Música
Hospital São João
Fânzeres
Carolina Michaelis
Marquês
Faria Guimarães
Estádio do Dragão
Trindade
Campanhã
Guimarães & Braga
Bolhão
Lapa
Campo 24 de Agosto
Heroísmo
Aliados
São Bento
São Bento
Batalha
Ribeira
Jardim do Morro
General Torres
Câmara Gaia
João de Deus
D. João II
Lisboa
Santo Ovídio
A Communicarta Style45 design
© Communicarta Ltd 2011 UDN.2a
Map user Ref: WZFG/PG/OPO/2011/2
Research and design by Robin Woods

There are currently three tram routes operating in Porto: 1, 18 and 22. The venerable vehicles (running 09.30–19.00 daily) are an attraction in themselves. A funicular runs from Rua Augusto Rosa to the riverfront beneath the Dom Luís I bridge.
Metro ⓦ www.metro-porto.pt
Buses and trams (in Porto) ⓦ www.stcp.pt

To get out of town, Porto has no central bus station. Consult one of the tourist offices (see page 135) for details. However, the local train system is pleasant, punctual and generally the best way to travel to nearby towns. Fares are low; buy tickets either at counters or from machines. You can catch local trains at either S Bento or Campanhã stations.

There are taxi ranks in Porto's main squares, at S Bento station and at several other locations. Taxi fares are moderate and metered (expect to pay about €5 for a journey in the city centre). Your hotel and restaurants will also call taxis for you.

Car hire

Portugal has fairly low car-hire rates, but check whether it's cheaper to book your car with your plane or train ticket. However, you should only need to hire a car (minimum age 23) if you want to travel outside Porto.
A A Castanheira Budget Lda ⓐ Avenida da Boavista 918 ⓣ 226 065 256 ⓦ www.budget.pt
Auto Jardim ⓐ Rua Guerra Junqueiro 634 ⓣ 226 053 197 ⓦ www.auto-jardim.com

The colourful houses and restaurants of the Cais da Ribeira

THE CITY OF

Porto

The World Heritage area & Vila Nova de Gaia

Porto started lobbying for UNESCO World Heritage status in 1993, and the distinction was awarded in 1996. The classified area is essentially the medieval borough located within the 14th-century city wall, parts of which still exist. It includes the oldest buildings in Porto, and newer ones such as the old stock exchange and the Dom Luís I bridge. It starts just south of the city's main square, Praça da Liberdade, and encompasses the Ribeira area, down to the Douro. It also stretches across the river to Vila Nova de Gaia, to include the Mosteiro da Serra do Pilar. The narrow cobbled streets of old houses wind down the steep hill, and can seem rundown at first – with washing hung out to dry, and buildings not in the best state of repair – before you take in the vibrant colours of the houses, and the lively bars and restaurants of Cais da Ribeira. Many buildings are rent-controlled, so landlords have had little incentive to keep them in good repair. All that is changing, however, as the area becomes increasingly gentrified. Its buildings are slowly being restored yet the sense of community is still palpable. Walking is really the only option, given the steep, narrow streets and limited bus services. There is only one metro station (S Bento), but taxis are also an option.

Vila Nova de Gaia (known simply as Gaia locally) is technically a separate municipality to Porto proper. But no trip to Porto is complete without a visit to the monastery and port lodges, as well as the many quayside restaurants and bars.

SIGHTS & ATTRACTIONS

The main attraction is simply wandering around, as you head past a range of fascinating buildings from different periods down to the Douro for eating, drinking and cruising options.

Cais da Ribeira (Ribeira Quay)

The colourful quayside and the streets behind it were Porto's original site and the hub of the city's seafaring and commercial activities before the wealthy merchants who flourished there gradually moved out to live higher up the hill. By the end of the 19th century the area had fallen into decline, but now it bustles with tourists instead. Restaurants nestle on the quayside, often within ancient arches. To the west of the quay is the small

Classic Ribeira façade

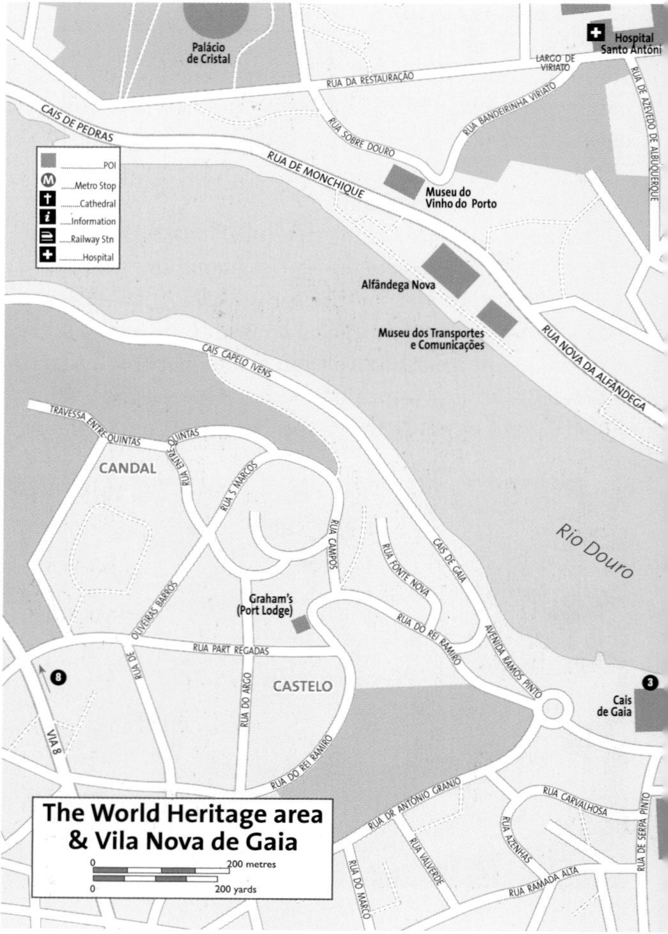

The World Heritage area & Vila Nova de Gaia

0 200 metres
0 200 yards

POI
Metro Stop
Cathedral
Information
Railway Stn
Hospital

Palácio de Cristal
Hospital Santo Antóni
Largo de Viriato
Rua da Restauração
Rua de Azevedo de Albuquerque
Rua Bandeirinha Viriato
Cais de Pedras
Rua Sobre Douro
Rua de Monchique
Museu do Vinho do Porto
Alfândega Nova
Museu dos Transportes e Comunicações
Rua Nova da Alfândega
Cais Capelo Ivens
Travessa Entre-Quintas
Rua Entre-Quintas
Candal
Rua S. Marcos
Rua Campos
Rio Douro
Rua Fonte Nova
Cais de Gaia
Oliveiras Barros
Rua de
Graham's (Port Lodge)
Rua do Rei Ramiro
Avenida Ramos Pinto
Rua Part Regadas
8
3
Cais de Gaia
Castelo
Rua do Argo
Via 8
Rua do Rei Ramiro
Rua Dr António Granjo
Rua Carvalhosa
Rua Azenhas
Rua de Serpa Pinto
Rua Valverde
Rua do Marco
Rua Ramada Alta

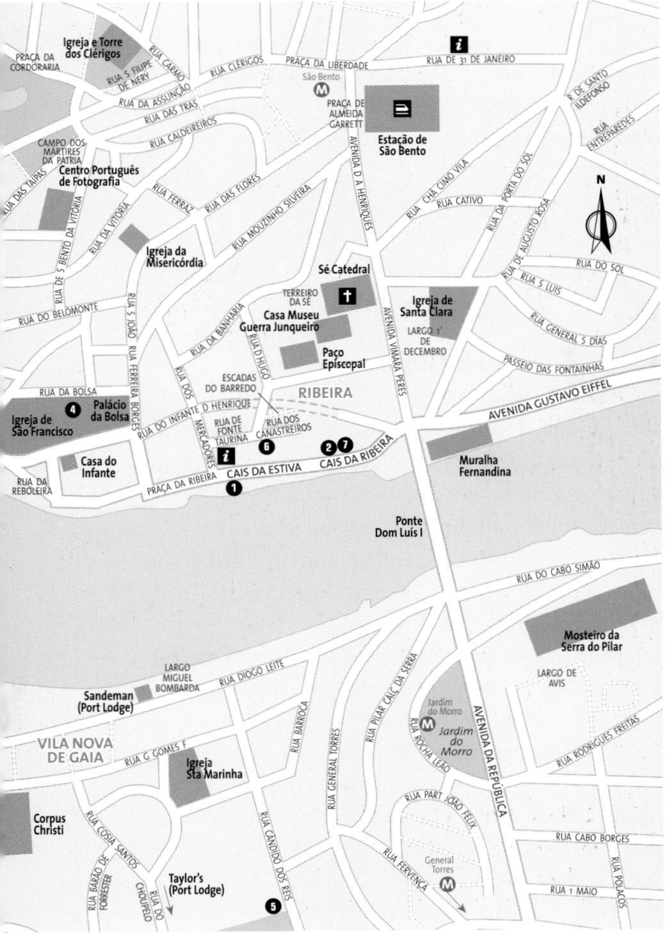

Igreja e Torre dos Clérigos
Praça da Cordoaria
Rua Carmo
Rua S Filipe de Nery
Rua Clérigos
Praça da Liberdade
Rua de 31 de Janeiro
São Bento
Rua da Assunção
Rua das Tras
Praça de Almeida Garrett
Estação de São Bento
R. de Santo Ildefonso
Rua Entreparedes
Rua Caldeireiros
Campo dos Martires da Patria
Rua das Taipas
Centro Português de Fotografia
Rua Ferraz
Rua das Flores
Rua Mouzinho Silveira
Avenida D A Henriques
Rua Chã Cimo Vila
Rua Cativo
Rua da Porta do Sol
Rua de Augusto Rosa
N
Rua de S Bento da Vitória
Rua da Vitória
Igreja da Misericórdia
Sé Catedral
Rua do Sol
Rua S Luis
Terreiro da Sé
Casa Museu Guerra Junqueiro
Igreja de Santa Clara
Rua do Belomonte
Rua S João
Rua Ferreira Borges
Rua da Banharia
Rua D Hugo
Largo 1º de Decembro
Avenida Vimara Peres
Rua General S Dias
Paço Episcopal
Passeio das Fontainhas
Rua dos Mercadores
Escadas do Barredo
Ribeira
Rua da Bolsa
Palácio da Bolsa
Igreja de São Francisco
Rua do Infante D Henrique
Rua de Fonte Taurina
Rua dos Canastreiros
Avenida Gustavo Eiffel
Casa do Infante
Cais da Estiva
Cais da Ribeira
Muralha Fernandina
Rua da Reboleira
Praça da Ribeira
Ponte Dom Luís I
Rua do Cabo Simão
Mosteiro da Serra do Pilar
Largo Miguel Bombarda
Rua Diogo Leite
Sandeman (Port Lodge)
Rua Pilar Calç da Serra
Largo de Avis
Jardim do Morro
Rua Barroca
Rua General Torres
Rua Rocha Leão
Avenida da República
Vila Nova de Gaia
Rua G Gomes F
Igreja Sta Marinha
Rua Rodrigues Freitas
Rua Part João Félix
Corpus Christi
Rua Cosia Santos
Rua Cândido dos Reis
Rua Cabo Borges
Rua Fervença
General Torres
Rua Barão de Forrester
Rua do Choupelo
Taylor's (Port Lodge)
Rua 1 Maio
Rua Polacos

square, Praça da Ribeira, originally medieval, but much of it dating from the neoclassical period. To the east is spectacular Ponte Dom Luís I, built in 1886. A funicular now runs from the foot of the bridge to near the cathedral and the metro runs along its upper level, giving unbeatable views of the Douro, Ribeira and Gaia. In the streets behind the waterfront, look out for a 14th-century house in Rua de D Hugo, the 13th-century building at No 5 Rua de Baixo near the Escadas do Barredo, and No 59 Rua da Reboleira, which almost certainly dates from the 14th century.

Estação de São Bento (São Bento Station)
The station was built in the early 20th century on the site of the convent of São Bento de Avé-Maria, and is worth popping into for a look at the 20,000 *azulejos* (tiles) in the entrance hall, which were designed in 1930 by the painter Jorge Colaço. They depict scenes from the history of railways and transport, and events in Portuguese history. The station is also a good place to get a taxi. ⓐ Praça de Almeida Garrett

Igreja da Misericórdia (Church of Our Lady of Mercy)
Building of this church started in 1555, with the interior tiles designed in 1629–30; the rococo façade dates from 1750. The small museum attached to the church, Santa Casa da Misericórdia, contains one of the finest paintings in the city, *Fons Vitae* (*Fountain of Life*), of the Flemish school, believed to have been painted in 1520. Rua das Flores was once a place of gold- and silversmiths, and is now full of interesting small shops. The houses date from the 18th century. ⓐ Rua das Flores 5 ⓣ 222 074 710 ⓦ www.scmp.pt

Church: 08.00–12.00, 14.30–17.30 Tues–Sun (Sept–July); museum: 09.30–12.00, 14.00–17.30 Mon–Fri Metro: D to S Bento Admission charge for museum

Igreja de Santa Clara (Church of St Clare)
This charming church was originally an early 15th-century Franciscan convent. The building has Gothic and Baroque elements and a Renaissance portal. Have a look at the 18th-century carved, gilded woodwork inside. Largo 1° de Decembro 222 054 837 09.30–11.30, 15.00–19.00 Mon–Fri Metro: D to S Bento

Igreja de São Francisco (Church of St Francis)
If you only have time to visit one church in Porto, make it this one by the side of the Palácio da Bolsa. It's deconsecrated now and was declared a National Monument in 1984. One of the few existing medieval buildings in Porto, it was built for the Franciscans in the 14th century in the Gothic style with a rose window, but the main attraction is the highly ornate Baroque interior. There is also a small museum in the catacombs, with furniture and a collection of sacred objects. The human bones in the ossuary date from the days before public cemeteries were introduced in Portugual in the 19th century. Rua do Infante D Henrique 222 062 100 09.00–20.00 (July & Aug); 09.00–19.00 (June, Sept & Oct); 09.00–18.00 (Feb–May); 09.00–17.30 (Nov–Jan) Metro: D to S Bento; tram: 1 to Infante Admission charge

Igreja e Torre dos Clérigos (Clérigos Church & Tower)
Just inside the northern part of the UNESCO area, the Baroque church and its tower were built between 1732 and 1773. From the

top of the 75-m (248-ft)-high tower you get great views of the city. The steps are broad and easy to negotiate, with several views on the way up – be careful though, they're through large openings. Note the unusual elliptical nave in the church. ⓐ Rua S Filipe de Nery ⓣ 222 001 729 ◷ Church: 08.45–12.30, 15.30–19.00 Mon–Sat, 10.00–13.00 Sun; tower: 09.30–13.00, 14.00–19.00 (Apr–Oct); 10.00–12.00, 14.00–17.00 (Nov–Mar) Ⓜ Metro: D to S Bento ⓘ Admission charge for tower

Mosteiro da Serra do Pilar (Monastery of Serra do Pilar)
Vila Nova de Gaia's main landmark was founded in the 16th century, and this monastery, with a circular church and cloister (most unusual in Portugal), was once the HQ of the future Duke of Wellington. At the beginning of the 20th century, the military connection continued when it became an army barracks. It is still under army control, and the church is difficult to visit (except by arrangement with the tourist office) other than for Mass on Sunday mornings. The terrace, however, is open to the public, and affords perhaps the best views of Porto. ⓐ Largo de Avis ⓣ 223 795 385 Ⓜ Metro: D to Jardim do Morro

Palácio da Bolsa (Stock Exchange Palace)
Just up the hill from the Ribeira waterfront, dominating the western side of the Rua do Infante Dom Henrique is the splendid neoclassical former stock exchange building: construction began in 1842 on the site of the old São Francisco monastery. The lavishly embellished interior has rooms and public areas decorated in a variety of styles – including a glass-roofed courtyard, the Pátio das Nações, with Roman-inspired mosaic floor and carved granite

and marble staircase. The highlight is the extravagant Salão Árabe (Arabian Hall). Although you can enter the building without paying, you can only visit the rooms with a guided tour. In the square itself you will see a monument to Henry the Navigator; to the north, an old market, Mercado Ferreira Borges, is now a venue for events. There is a tourist office to the south of the square, and the late-17th-century church of São Nicolau, with its blue-tiled front.
Rua Ferreira Borges 223 399 000 www.palaciodabolsa.pt
09.00–19.00 (Apr–Oct); 09.00–13.00, 14.00–18.00 (Nov–Mar)
Metro: D to S Bento; tram: 1 E to Infante

The Dom Luís I bridge spans the Douro

The port lodges of Vila Nova de Gaia

There are over a dozen lodges – where port is aged and matured – owned by shippers on or near the quayside of Vila Nova de Gaia. Almost all of them offer guided tours and tastings: any admission charge is deducted from the price of what you buy. And they're obviously a good place to buy port. The majority of the firms (many of them originally British) were once family owned, but are now run by international drinks companies. Their names are prominently displayed outside the lodges, and illuminated at night. From Ribeira or central Porto, you'll have to walk across the Dom Luís I bridge, take a taxi or take the metro to Jardim do Morro and then walk down. A more colourful alternative is to be ferried across the Douro. Try to get to a lodge at least 30 minutes before its closing time. There are several good ones to visit, but three of the best are:

Graham's Established in the early 19th century, and run by the Symington family for several generations. The family is unusual in owning its own vineyards. They also own other brands such as Dow's and Warre's. The lodge, still working, is behind the quayside, up a hill. The tours are very informative, with tastings of high-quality port; you can also watch a film about port-making. The terrace offers very good views of Porto. ⓐ Quinta do Agro 514, Rua do Rei Ramiro ⓣ 223 776 330 ⓦ www.symington.com ⓗ 09.30–18.00 daily (May–Sept); 09.30–13.00, 14.00–17.30 Mon–Fri (Oct–Apr) ⓘ Closed public holidays

Sandeman On the quayside, and the most conveniently located. The firm (now Portuguese-owned) was founded by Scotsman

George Sandeman in 1790, and is famous for its 'Don' symbol, of a man in a black cloak, one of the first trademark images ever created (in 1928). There's a port museum, a bottle collection and a gift shop. The tour takes around 30 minutes and includes a good film about the making of port. ⓐ Largo Miguel Bombarda 3 ⓣ 223 740 533/4 ⓦ www.sandeman.com ⓛ 10.00–12.30, 14.00–18.00 (Mar–Oct); 09.30–12.30, 14.00–17.30 (Nov–Feb) ⓘ Admission charge for tour only

Taylor's Founded over 300 years ago, and producing some of the best port around, the firm is still independently owned. After the tour (which is free) and a tasting in the elegant library, you can visit the shop or have lunch in the restaurant – outside in the garden, with its view of Porto, in summer. ⓐ Rua do Choupelo 250 ⓣ 223 742 800 ⓦ www.taylor.pt ⓛ 10.00–18.00 Mon–Fri (Sept–June); 10.00–18.00 Mon–Sat (July & Aug)

Sé Catedral (Cathedral)

The imposing cathedral, on its dominating hill, was the heart of Porto in the Middle Ages, and is the city's most important historical building. Construction started in the 12th century, in the Romanesque style; the Gothic vestry and the cloister date from the 14th century. Changes made in the 18th century include a silver altarpiece, as well as cloister murals by Nicolau Nasoni. Note also the Baroque *azulejos* decorating the cloister, the crypt and the staircase to the fine chapter house. On the terrace, to the south of the cathedral, is the grand bishop's palace, originally built in the 13th century, but heavily remodelled in the late 18th century. To the north is the Torre Medieval. Medieval

Sé Cathedral traces its origins back to the 12th century

tower remains were discovered in the 1940s, but this is a reconstruction, moved about 15 m (48 ft) from the original site in the 1950s, and is now the place to book tours through Porto Tours (see page 34). ⓐ Terreiro da Sé ⓣ 222 050 028 ◷ Cathedral: 08.45–12.30, 14.30–19.00 (Apr–Oct); 08.45–12.30, 14.30–18.00 (Nov–Mar); cloisters: 09.00–12.15, 14.30–18.00 Mon–Sat (Apr–Oct); 09.00–12.15, 14.30–17.15 Mon–Sat (Nov–Mar) Ⓜ Metro: D to S Bento ❗ Admission charge for cloisters

CULTURE

Casa do Infante (The House of the Prince)

Once a medieval customs house, dating from 1325, this is the supposed birthplace of Prince Henry the Navigator in 1394. The unpromising 17th-century exterior belies a modern museum in the older part of the building featuring the site's and city's history from Roman times (note the impressive mosaic floor near the ticket desk), using an interactive model of medieval Porto, multimedia, displays of artefacts including ceramics and glass, as well as allusions to the life of Henry the Navigator. Temporary exhibitions are also held there. Last admission 30 minutes before closing times. ⓐ Rua Nova da Alfândega 10 ⓣ 222 060 400 ⓦ www.cm-porto.pt ◷ 10.00–12.30, 14.00–17.30 Tues–Sat, 14.00–17.30 Sun Ⓜ Metro: D to S Bento ❗ Admission charge

Casa Museu Guerra Junqueiro (Guerra Junqueiro House and Museum)

This Baroque house, built in the 18th century, was once the home of the poet Guerra Junqueiro (1850–1923) and contains his collection of art, textiles and artefacts including Islamic works and ceramics. A charming place to visit. ⓐ Rua D Hugo 32 ⓣ 222 003 689 ⓦ www.cm-porto.pt ⓛ 10.00–12.30, 14.00–17.30 Tues–Sat, 14.00–17.30 Sun ⓜ Metro: D to S Bento ⓘ Admission charge

Centro Português de Fotografia (Portuguese Centre for Photography)
This stately yellow building, dating from 1765, was once a prison, but is now the national photographic centre, displaying an archive of old photos of Porto and Lisbon, and exhibits to do with the history of photography. Look out for the high-quality temporary exhibitions. ⓐ Campo dos Mártires da Pátria ⓣ 222 076 310 ⓛ 15.00–18.00 Tues–Fri, 15.00–19.00 Sat, Sun & public holidays ⓜ Metro: D to S Bento ⓘ Free admission except for special events

RETAIL THERAPY

Artesanato dos Clérigos Traditional Portuguese craft objects and regional costumes. ⓐ Rua da Assunção 33–34 ⓣ 222 000 257 ⓛ 09.30–12.30, 14.30–19.00 Mon–Fri, 09.30–13.00 Sat (Nov–May); 09.30–12.30, 14.30–19.00 Mon–Fri, 09.30–19.00 Sat (June–Oct)

Casa das Cestinhas One of the best places to go for local handicrafts. ⓐ Cais da Ribeira 34 ⓣ 222 001 690 ⓛ 09.00–19.00 Mon–Sat

CRAT (Centro Regional de Artes Tradicionais) In a 17th-century building, this is the official centre for traditional local

workmanship. ⓐ Rua da Reboleira 37 ⓣ 223 320 201 ⓛ 10.00–13.00, 14.00–18.00 Mon–Fri

Galeria de Artesanato O Galo High-quality ceramics by local designers. ⓐ Rua Mouzinho da Silveira 68 ⓣ 223 325 294 ⓛ 09.30–12.30, 13.30–19.00 Mon–Fri, 09.30–13.00 Sat

Garrafeira Clériporto A good place to buy port, near the Clérigos Tower. ⓐ Rua da Assunção 38 ⓣ 222 038 026 ⓛ 09.30–13.00, 14.30–19.30, Mon–Fri, 09.30–13.00 Sat

Portosigns In a cellar opposite the Casa do Infante, this shop stocks an eclectic range of local products and souvenirs. ⓐ Rua da Alfândega 17 ⓣ 220 160 559 ⓦ www.portosigns.pt ⓛ 10.00–20.00 Mon–Sat, 14.00–19.00 Sun

TAKING A BREAK

Café do Cais £ ❶ This recent, and very popular, addition to Porto's café scene is just along from the Ribeira quay. It's basically a glass box (though it also has a terrace) from which you can sip your coffee and look at the port lodges of Gaia. ⓐ Cais da Estiva ⓣ 222 088 385 ⓛ Varies seasonally

A Canastra da Ribeira £ ❷ A small restaurant with stone walls and beamed ceilings, where you can also sit outdoors and get a drink outside dining hours. Try the fried octopus or the sardines. ⓐ Cais da Ribeira 37 ⓣ 222 080 180 ⓛ 12.00–22.30 (summer); 12.00–15.30, 18.30–22.30 (winter) ⓜ Metro: D to S Bento

Bogani Café £–££ ❸ One of the trendiest places in Gaia, with Philippe Starck furnishings. Right on the quay. ⓐ Cais de Gaia ⓣ 223 747 0700 ⓛ Varies seasonally

O Comercial ££ ❹ In the Palácio da Bolsa, with its fine interior. Very good Portuguese food in a formal setting – and a view of the church of São Francisco. ⓐ Palácio da Bolsa, Rua Ferreira Borges ⓣ 223 322 019 ⓛ 12.30–15.00, 20.00–23.00 Mon–Sat Ⓜ Metro: D to S Bento

AFTER DARK

RESTAURANTS

Adega e Presuntaria Transmontana II ££ ❺ Grilled and smoked meat is the speciality in this popular, stone-walled Gaia restaurant. ⓐ Rua Candido dos Reis 132 ⓣ 223 597 792 ⓛ 12.30–15.00, 19.30–23.00

Chez Lapin ££ ❻ There's been a restaurant in these former stables on the Ribeira quay since 1910. You can eat outside, downstairs (decorated with football memorabilia) or upstairs (with its old lampshades, and graffiti and business cards, memos, etc on the walls). Service is friendly, and the food excellent – try the roasted octopus. ⓐ Rua dos Canastreiros 42 ⓣ 222 006 418 ⓛ 12.30–15.00, 19.00–23.30 Ⓜ Metro: D to S Bento

D Tonho ££ ❼ Rather more expensive than many of Ribeira's eateries, this restaurant is a fashionable spot belonging to the Portuguese pop star Rui Veloso. The modern interior, with

its exposed granite walls, totally belies the rather unimpressive exterior. High-quality, creative and well-presented food features ingredients such as rabbit (with coriander) and kid in various guises. There's also a bar downstairs which doubles as a dining area for smokers. ⓐ Cais da Ribeira 13–15 ⓣ 222 004 307 ⓛ 12.30–14.45, 19.30–23.15 ⓜ Metro: D to S Bento

Horta dos Reis ££ ❽ A favourite for local parties with its gardens and view from Gaia over to Ribeira; best visited in summer. A lively atmosphere and particularly good fish and seafood. ⓐ Rua Camilo Castelo Branco 947 ⓣ 223 770 324 ⓛ 12.30–15.00, 19.30–23.00 Mon–Fri, 19.30–23.00 Sat

BARS & CLUBS

Aniki-Bóbó One of the most fashionable clubs in town, often with live music. ⓐ Rua da Fonte Taurina 36–38 ⓣ 223 324 619 ⓛ 21.00–02.00 Tues–Sat

Hard Club In Gaia, and one of the city's main live music venues. ⓐ Cais de Gaia 1158 ⓣ 223 744 755 ⓛ 22.00–04.00 Wed–Sat

Ribeirinha One of the oldest bars in Ribeira. It's often crowded and always cheerful. ⓐ Rua de São João 70–72 ⓣ 223 322 572 ⓛ 22.00–02.00

Ryan's Irish Pub Just what the name says and is often packed. ⓐ Rua do Infante D Henrique 18 ⓣ 222 005 366 ⓛ Late nights: 10.00–02.00 Thur & Sun, 21.00–04.00 Fri, 17.00–04.00 Sat ⓘ There's a cover charge after 23.00

The city centre

The city centre is the heart of Porto's commercial life, and the main shopping district. The attractive squares and streets (several of them pedestrianised), with their mixture of different architectural styles, are well worth wandering around to get a feel for the life of modern Porto. It's also where you will find banks, some of the main performance venues and two of the city's three tourist offices. And you can't fail to notice the area's characteristic patterned pavements, made of limestone and basalt – and slippery in the rain.

SIGHTS & ATTRACTIONS

There are few formal attractions in the city centre, but many interesting 19th- and 20th-century buildings, though some of those dating from the 1950s to the 1970s are pretty functional and now appear somewhat faded.

The focal point here is the mainly neoclassical and Art Nouveau Avenida dos Aliados, with one square, the Praça do General Humberto, at the north end and another, the Praça da Liberdade, at the south. The north end is dominated by the **Câmara Municipal** (Town Hall; also known as Paços do Concelho), which may look as if it's been there for centuries, but was completed only in 1957. The equestrian statue in Praça da Liberdade is of the 19th-century King Pedro IV, unveiled in 1866.

To the east of Praça do General Humberto is the colourful two-tiered, mainly wrought-iron, 19th-century **Mercado do Bolhão** (Bolhão food market). A little further to the east is the Rua de

Santa Catarina, the main shopping street. Look out for the Café Majestic at No 112, with its fine 1920s interior, and the striking exterior tiles of the simple, early-18th-century Capela das Almas at No 428. The tiles on this chapel date only from 1929 (restored in 1982) and depict the lives of Saints Francis and Catherine. The street also has a major shopping centre. In the Rua de Passos Manuel is the **Coliseu Theatre**, a former cinema, and now a major venue for high-profile performances. A little further to the south is the pleasant Praça da Batalha, with its fountain, where you will find the **Teatro Nacional de São João**, built in 1909.

To the west of the Praça da Liberdade, near the Hospital Santo António, is a small park, the Jardim da Cordoaria. The area also has several buildings which are part of the university.

The Praça da Liberdade is a focal point for the city centre

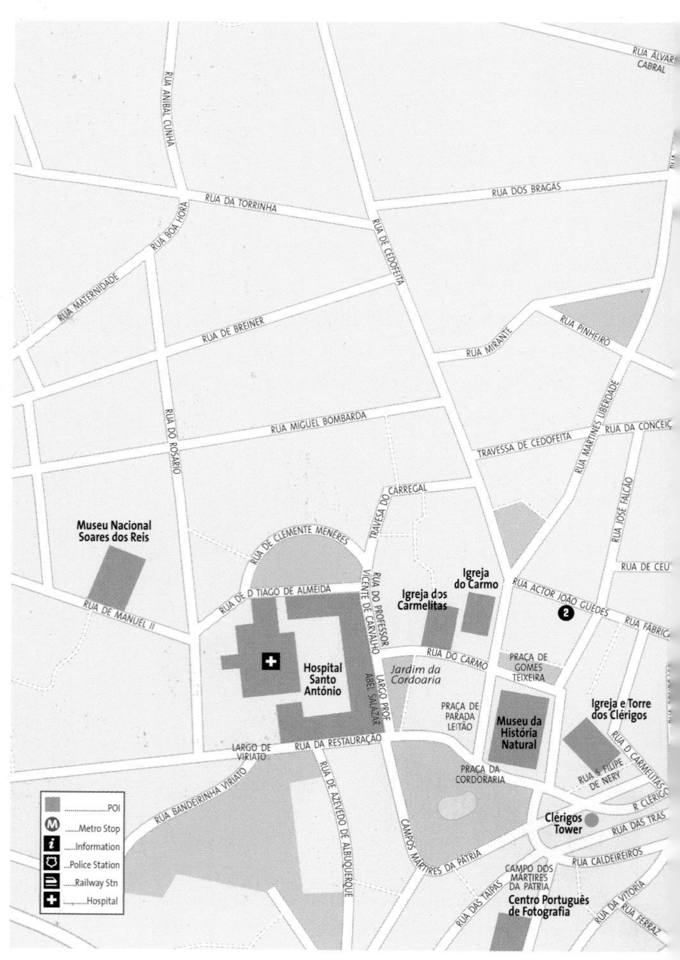

RUA ÁLVAR CABRAL
RUA ANIBAL CUNHA
RUA DOS BRAGAS
RUA DA TORRINHA
RUA BOA HORA
RUA DE CEDOFEITA
RUA MATERNIDADE
RUA DE BREINER
RUA PINHEIRO
RUA MIRANTE
RUA MARTINES LIBERDADE
RUA MIGUEL BOMBARDA
RUA DA CONCEIÇ
TRAVESSA DE CEDOFEITA
RUA DO ROSÁRIO
TRAVESSA DO CARREGAL
RUA JOSÉ FALCÃO
Museu Nacional Soares dos Reis
RUA DE CLEMENTE MENÉRES
RUA DE CEU
Igreja do Carmo
Igreja dos Carmelitas
RUA DE D TIAGO DE ALMEIDA
RUA DO PROFESSOR VICENTE DE CARVALHO
RUA ACTOR JOÃO GUEDES
RUA DE MANUEL II
RUA FÁBRICA
RUA DO CARMO
PRAÇA DE GOMES TEIXEIRA
Hospital Santo António
Jardim da Cordoaria
LARGO PROF ABEL SALAZAR
PRAÇA DE PARADA LEITÃO
Museu da História Natural
Igreja e Torre dos Clérigos
RUA D CARMELITAS
LARGO DE VIRIATO
RUA DA RESTAURAÇÃO
PRAÇA DA CORDOARIA
RUA S FILIPE DE NERY
RUA BANDEIRINHA VIRIATO
RUA DE AZEVEDO DE ALBUQUERQUE
R CLÉRIGO
Clérigos Tower
RUA DAS TRAS
POI
Metro Stop
Information
Police Station
Railway Stn
Hospital
CAMPOS MÁRTIRES DA PÁTRIA
RUA CALDEIREIROS
CAMPO DOS MÁRTIRES DA PÁTRIA
RUA DAS TAIPAS
Centro Português de Fotografia
RUA DA VITÓRIA
RUA FERRAZ

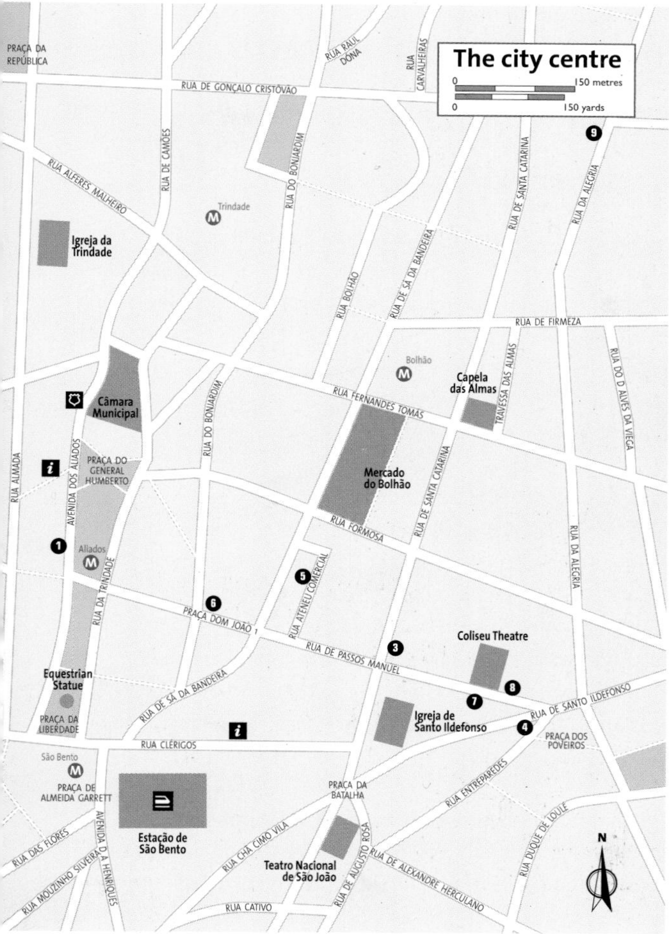

The city centre

0 150 metres
0 150 yards

PRAÇA DA REPÚBLICA
RUA RAUL DÓNA
RUA CARVALHEIRAS
RUA DE GONÇALO CRISTÓVÃO
RUA DE CAMÕES
RUA DO BONJARDIM
RUA ALFERES MALHEIRO
Trindade
Igreja da Trindade
RUA DE SANTA CATARINA
RUA DA ALEGRIA
RUA BOLHÃO
RUA DE SÁ DA BANDEIRA
RUA DE FIRMEZA
Bolhão
Câmara Municipal
Capela das Almas
TRAVESSA DAS ALMAS
RUA DO D ALVES DA VIEGA
RUA FERNANDES TOMÁS
RUA DO BONJARDIM
RUA ALMADA
AVENIDA DOS ALIADOS
PRAÇA DO GENERAL HUMBERTO
Mercado do Bolhão
RUA DE SANTA CATARINA
RUA FORMOSA
RUA DA ALEGRIA
Aliados
RUA ATENEU COMERCIAL
RUA DA TRINDADE
PRAÇA DOM JOÃO I
RUA DE PASSOS MANUEL
Coliseu Theatre
Equestrian Statue
RUA DE SÁ DA BANDEIRA
PRAÇA DA LIBERDADE
Igreja de Santo Ildefonso
RUA DE SANTO ILDEFONSO
PRAÇA DOS POVEIROS
RUA CLÉRIGOS
São Bento
PRAÇA DE ALMEIDA GARRETT
Estação de São Bento
PRAÇA DA BATALHA
RUA ENTREPAREDES
RUA DAS FLORES
RUA MOUZINHO SILVEIRA
AVENIDA D A HENRIQUES
RUA CHÃ CIMO VILA
Teatro Nacional de São João
RUA DE AUGUSTO ROSA
RUA DE ALEXANDRE HERCULANO
RUA DUQUE DE LOULÉ
RUA CATIVO
N

Hospital Santo António

The exterior of this imposing building, with its six Doric columns, is well worth a look. One of the city's main hospitals, built 1790–1825, it was designed by English architect John Carr, who was the first to introduce the British neo-Palladian style to Porto. Ⓐ Largo Prof Abel Salazar Ⓜ Metro: D to S Bento

Igreja dos Carmelitas (Church of the Carmelites)

This former convent, built in the early 17th century with considerable alterations made a century later, includes a main chapel built by master mason António da Silva. The interior is mainly in the rococo style. The rather solemn façade is mid-18th century. Ⓐ Rua do Carmo Ⓣ 222 050 279 Ⓛ 09.30–13.00, 14.00–19.00 daily Ⓜ Metro: D to S Bento

Igreja do Carmo (Carmel Church)

This former monastery is one of the outstanding rococo buildings in Porto. Of especial interest are the unusual balcony on the main façade, and the richly decorated *azulejos*, on the side of the building, which refer to the life of the Virgin Mary. The pediment at the top of the main façade features figures representing the four Evangelists. Step inside to admire the ornate interior. Ⓐ Rua do Carmo Ⓣ 222 078 400 Ⓛ 08.00–12.00, 14.00–17.00 Mon–Fri, 08.00–12.00 Sat, 07.30–13.00 Sun Ⓜ Metro: D to S Bento

Igreja de Santo Ildefonso (Church of St Ildefonsus)

In the Praça da Batalha, it's worth quickly popping into this peaceful and essentially simple church built from 1709–39, with its polygonal nave (with a wooden ceiling), Baroque elements in

The 18th-century Capela das Almas on Rua de Santa Catarina

the interior and exterior tiles dating from 1932. ⓐ Praça da Batalha ⓣ 222 004 366 ⓑ 09.00–12.00, 15.00–17.30 Mon–Fri, 09.00–12.00, 15.00–18.00 Sat ⓜ Metro: D to S Bento

CULTURE

Museu da História Natural (Natural History Museum)

This fine neoclassical building was completed in the late 19th century, and is now part of the university's Faculty of Sciences. There are two exhibition halls open to the public: Archaeology and Palaeontology, and Mineralogy. ⓐ Praça de Gomes Teixeira ⓣ 223 401 400 ⓑ Archaeology and Palaeontology: 10.00–12.00 Mon–Fri; Mineralogy: 14.30–16.30 Mon–Fri ⓜ Metro: D to S Bento

Museu Nacional Soares dos Reis (Soares dos Reis Museum)

Porto's main museum: home to collections of both visual and decorative arts, and pleasantly bright and unstuffy. Formerly the Palácio dos Carrancas, once a wealthy merchant's residence and built at the end of the 18th century, it became a royal palace in the mid-19th century and later Portugal's first fine arts museum. Paintings and sculptures on the first floor (including the work of 19th-century sculptor António Soares dos Reis, after whom the museum is named) are by Portuguese artists from the 19th century to the mid-20th century, as well as foreigners who produced works in Portugal. Look out for old views of Porto and the Douro, and the works of Henrique Pousão; some sculptures date from as far back as the medieval period. The decorative arts section on the second floor includes ceramics, glass, jewellery, textiles and furniture, both Portuguese and foreign, dating from the 17th to the 20th centuries. The museum also holds major temporary exhibitions. The attractive tiled courtyard is used as a café in summer. ⓐ Rua D Manuel II 44 ⓣ 223 393 770

The pretty pink façade of the Museu Nacional Soares dos Reis

ⓦ www.ipmuseus.pt ⓛ 14.00–18.00 Tues, 10.00–18.00 Wed–Sun ⓝ Bus: 3, 6, 20, 24, 35, 37, 52, 78, 500 to Miragaia ⓘ Admission charge (free until 14.00 Sun & public holidays)

RETAIL THERAPY

Arcadia Established in 1933, one of the best places to buy pastries, chocolate and confectionery. ⓐ Rua Almada 63 ⓣ 222 001 518 ⓛ 09.30–19.00 Mon–Fri, 09.30–13.00 Sat

Armazém dos Linhos Founded in the late 19th century, selling linen and decorative woven fabrics. ⓐ Rua de Passos Manuel 19 ⓣ 222 004 750 ⓛ 09.30–12.30, 14.30–19.00 Mon–Thur, 10.00–12.30, 14.30–19.00 Fri, 10.00–13.00 Sat

Canjirão Portuguese handicrafts. ⓐ Rua de Santo Ildefonso 215 ⓣ 222 008 523 ⓛ 10.00–12.15, 15.15–19.15 Mon–Fri, 10.00–13.00 Sat

Cerâmica Kico Craft objects, including ceramics. ⓐ Rua de Santa Catarina 212 ⓣ 222 059 162 ⓛ 10.00–19.30 Mon–Sat

Garrafeira do Carmo One of the city's best port and wine shops, with vintage port, some of which dates back to 1900. ⓐ Rua do Carmo 17–18 ⓣ 222 003 285 ⓛ 09.00–13.00, 14.00–19.00 Mon–Sat

Livraria Lello As much a sight as a bookshop. Over a century old, and with a stunning Art Nouveau interior, dominated by a grand wooden staircase, it specialises in art books (many in English)

as well as books about Porto and maps. There are a few tables upstairs where you can relax with a drink or a pastry. ⓐ Rua das Carmelitas 144 ⓣ 222 018 170 ⓛ 10.00–19.30 Mon–Sat

Memórias A good craft shop, near S Bento station. ⓐ Rua das Flores 18 ⓣ 222 085 726 ⓛ 09.30–12.30, 14.30–19.00 Mon–Fri, 10.00–13.00 Sat

A Pérola do Bolhão With a striking Art Nouveau façade, this food store – selling cheese, sausages, salt cod, port and other specialities – was founded in 1917 opposite the entrance to Bolhão market. ⓐ Rua Formosa 279 ⓣ 222 004 009 ⓛ 09.30–13.00, 15.00–19.30 Mon–Fri, 09.30–13.00 Sat

Via Catarina One of Porto's main shopping centres, selling mainly clothes. Bars and cafés on the top floor (level 4). ⓐ Rua de Santa Catarina 312–350 ⓣ 222 075 600 ⓛ Shops: 10.00–22.00; food outlets: 09.00–23.00

TAKING A BREAK

Café Guarany £ ❶ Founded in 1933, a musicians' haunt with live music in the evenings, and good-value food and drinks. Sit inside or out on the street. ⓐ Avenida dos Aliados 85–89 ⓣ 223 321 272 ⓛ 09.00–24.00 ⓜ Metro: D to Aliados

Café Progresso £ ❷ Opened in 1899, and a local institution. ⓐ Rua Actor João Guedes 5 ⓣ 223 322 647 ⓛ 07.00–19.00 Mon–Thur, 07.00–24.00 Fri & Sat ⓜ Metro: D to S Bento

Café Majestic £–££ ❸ Come to this famous café, with its 1920s interior and uniformed waiters, for a coffee and a pastry – or something a bit more substantial. ⓐ Rua de Santa Catarina 112 ⓣ 222 003 887 ⓑ 09.30–24.00 Mon–Sat ⓜ Metro: A, B, C, E to Bolhão

Ribeiro £–££ ❹ One of the best places for traditional food in the city centre, in a semi-rustic setting. Try the *bacalhau* (salt cod) or maybe the tripe if you're up to it. ⓐ Praça dos Poveiros 2 ⓣ 222 008 637 ⓑ 12.00–15.00, 19.00–23.00 ⓜ Metro: D to S Bento or A, B, C, E to Bolhão

AFTER DARK

RESTAURANTS

Abadia do Porto £ ❺ Large, simple and lively, serving straightforward local cuisine. ⓐ Rua Ateneu Comercial 22 ⓣ 222 008 757 ⓑ 12.00–23.00 Mon–Sat ⓜ Metro: D to Aliados

Café Concerto Rivoli £ ❻ A good, popular budget choice for Portuguese specialities. ⓐ Praça Dom João I ⓣ 223 392 200 ⓑ 12.30–15.00, 19.30–23.00 ⓜ Metro: D to Aliados

O Escondidinho ££ ❼ Well-prepared local food, particularly the fish and seafood. Also decent meat dishes, some from further afield. ⓐ Rua de Passos Manuel 142 ⓣ 222 001 079 ⓦ www.escondidinho.com.pt ⓑ 12.00–15.00, 19.00–23.00 ⓜ Metro: D to S Bento or Aliados

Tripeiro ££ ❽ Hearty local cuisine, including tripe, as the name suggests. ⓐ Rua de Passos Manuel 195 ⓣ 222 005 886 ◷ 12.00–15.00, 19.00–22.00 Mon–Sat Ⓝ Metro: D to S Bento or Aliados

Portucale £££ ❾ Generally considered one of the best restaurants in Porto (serving Portuguese cuisine and luxury ingredients) with a 13th-floor location, offering superb views as well as fine food. ⓐ Rua da Alegria 596 ⓣ 225 370 717 ◷ 12.30–14.30, 19.30–22.00 Ⓝ Metro: A, B, C, E to Bolhão

BARS & CLUBS

There are many bars in the area, though a lot of them close early. The two below are particularly good:

Cinema Batalha With two trendy bars and a terrace. ⓐ Praça da Batalha 47 ⓣ 222 011 913 ◷ 12.00–02.00 Mon–Thur, 12.00–04.00 Fri–Sun

Maus Hábitos A cultural centre with a restaurant and a lively bar. ⓐ Rua de Passos Manuel 178 (4th floor) ⓣ 222 087 268 ◷ 22.00–02.00 Wed, Thur & Sun, 22.00–04.00 Fri & Sat

West of the city centre

Many of Porto's most appealing museums and attractions are to the west of the city centre and the World Heritage area – either along the Douro or in the Boavista area. Both areas offer a striking contrast to crowded Ribeira and the bustling city centre. In Boavista, the roads and avenues are broad and leafy, with some of the best modern hotels and classy shops as well as the homes of Porto's wealthier inhabitants. In **Foz do Douro**, normally referred to simply as Foz, the riverside and the seashore are more like a resort area, with waterfront restaurants and cafés. The large villas lining the streets leading downhill are among the most exclusive in the city. Western Porto is currently not well served by the metro, except to the north, so you'll need to gear up for some serious walking or rely on buses or taxis.

SIGHTS & ATTRACTIONS

The Boavista area starts at the Rotunda da Boavista (officially called Praça Mouzinho de Albuquerque, a name rarely used), a busy roundabout, with a small park in the centre, 3 km (2 miles) northwest of Praça da Liberdade. The middle of the park is dominated by a tall column commemorating the Peninsular War (1808–14) and the victory over the French. It was actually built in 1951. Just to the west of the roundabout is the **Casa da Música**. Nearby are two shopping centres. The Avenida da Boavista runs 8 km (5 miles) from the Rotunda to the Atlantic and Foz do Douro, passing the Parque da Cidade – Porto's biggest green space. The equestrian statue near the sea is of the early-19th-

century king João VI looking towards Brazil. Along the avenue, note the grand late-19th-century houses built by returning Portuguese who had made their fortunes in Brazil. They often have palm trees in their gardens, planted to remind their owners of the New World. The area also has several fine 1930s houses, and cutting-edge modern buildings.

Around 2 km (1 mile) to the south of the Rotunda, and not far from the UNESCO area are a cluster of museums near the Douro, as well as the Palácio de Cristal park.

The Foz do Douro area is to the west of the concrete Ponte de Arrábida, with its 270-m (885-ft) span. There are few formal sights or attractions, but the area is particularly pleasant, with paths by the mouth of the river and the Atlantic where many people jog, small beaches (where you are advised not to swim) and lively nightlife in summer, particularly on the Avenida do Brasil and its continuation towards Ribeira, the Avenida de Dom Carlos I. The two forts on the coast are the **Castelo do Queijo**, at the end of the Avenida da Boavista, and **Castelo de São João da Foz**, to the southeast.

Casa da Música (House of Music)

After years of delay, the hugely impressive and spankingly modern polyhedron-shaped Casa da Música, designed by Dutch architect Rem Koolhaas, finally opened in 2005. Porto's concert hall and opera house is now the base of the Orquestra Nacional do Porto, and has fast become a major centre of local cultural life.
ⓐ Rotunda da Boavista ⓣ 220 120 220 ⓦ www.casadamusica.com
ⓑ Box office: 10.00–19.00 Mon–Sat, 10.00–18.00 Sun ⓝ Metro: A, B, C, E to Casa da Música

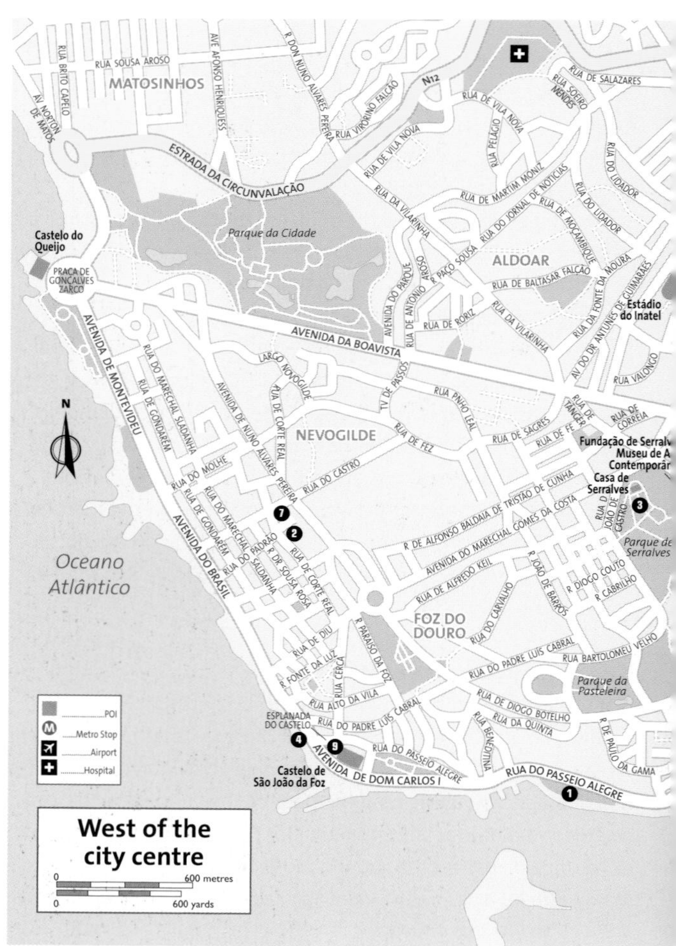
MATOSINHOS
ALDOAR
NEVOGILDE
FOZ DO DOURO
Parque da Cidade
Castelo do Queijo
Estádio do Inatel
Casa de Serralves
Parque de Serralves
Parque da Pasteleira
Castelo de São João da Foz
Oceano Atlântico
ESTRADA DA CIRCUNVALAÇÃO
AVENIDA DA BOAVISTA
AVENIDA DE MONTEVIDEU
AVENIDA DO BRASIL
AVENIDA DE DOM CARLOS I
RUA DO PASSEIO ALEGRE
POI
Metro Stop
Airport
Hospital
West of the city centre
600 metres
600 yards

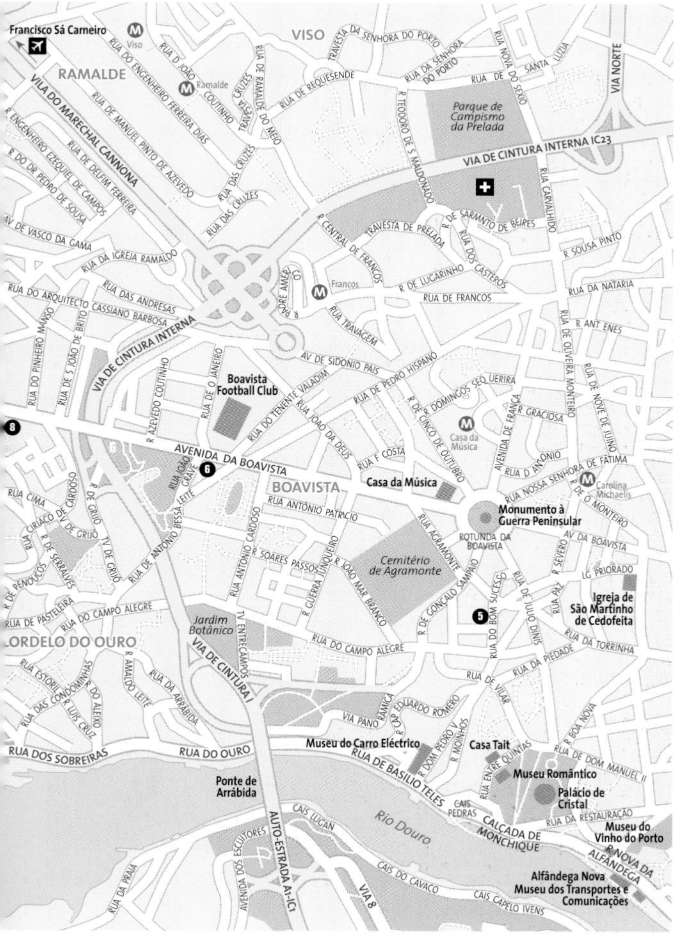
Francisco Sá Carneiro
Viso
VISO
RAMALDE
Ramalde
Travessa da Senhora do Porto
Rua da Senhora do Porto
Rua Nova do Sexto
Rua de Santa Luzia
Via Norte
Rua do Engenheiro Ferreira Dias
Rua D João Coutinho
Travessa Cruzes
Rua de Ramalde do Meio
Rua de Requesende
R Teodoro de S Maldonado
Parque de Campismo da Prelada
Via de Cintura Interna IC23
Vila do Marechal Cannona
Rua de Manuel Pinto de Azevedo
Rua das Cruzes
R Engenheiro Ezequiel de Campos
Rua de Delfim Ferreira
R do Dr Pedro de Sousa
Av de Vasco da Gama
Rua da Igreja Ramalde
R Central de Francos
Travessa de Prelada
R de Sarmento de Beires
Rua dos Castelos
Rua Carvalhido
R Sousa Pinto
Rua da Nataria
Francos
R de Lugarinho
Rua de Francos
R Padre Amer. Co
Rua Travagem
Rua do Arquitecto Cassiano Barbosa
Rua das Andresas
Via de Cintura Interna
Rua do Pinheiro Manso
Rua de S João de Brito
Rua de Oliveira Monteiro
R Ant Enes
Av de Sidónio Pais
Rua de Pedro Hispano
R Domingos Sequeira
Rua de Nove de Julho
R Azevedo Coutinho
Rua de O Janeiro
Boavista Football Club
Rua do Tenente Valadim
Rua João da Deus
R de Cinco de Outubro
Casa da Música
Avenida de França
R Graciosa
Avenida da Boavista
Rua João Grave
Rua F Costa
Rua D António
Rua Nossa Senhora de Fátima
Carolina Michaelis
R de O Monteiro
BOAVISTA
Rua António Patrício
Rua Cima
Rua Ciriaco de Cardoso
R de Griió
Tv de Griió
Rua de António Bessa Leite
Rua Agramonte
Monumento à Guerra Peninsular
Rotunda da Boavista
Av da Boavista
R Severo
LG Priorado
R de Serralves
R de Penoucos
Rua António Cardoso
R Soares Passos
R Guerra Junqueiro
R João Mar Branco
Cemitério de Agramonte
R de Gonçalo Sampaio
Rua do Bom Sucesso
Rua de Júlio Dinis
Rua Paz
Igreja de São Martinho de Cedofeita
Rua de Pasteleira
Rua do Campo Alegre
Jardim Botânico
Tv Entrecampos
Rua da Torrinha
LORDELO DO OURO
Rua Estoril
Rua das Condominhas
R Luís Cruz
R do Aleixo
R Amaldo Leite
Rua da Arrábida
Via de Cintura I
Rua de Vilar
Rua da Piedade
Via Panorâmica
R Cap Eduardo Romero
R Dom Pedro V
R Moinhos
R Boa Nova
Rua dos Sobreiras
Rua do Ouro
Museu do Carro Eléctrico
Casa Tait
Rua Entre Quintas
Rua de Dom Manuel II
Museu Romântico
Rua de Basílio Teles
Ponte de Arrábida
Palácio de Cristal
Cais Pedras
Rua da Restauração
Cais Lugan
Rio Douro
Calçada de Monchique
Museu do Vinho do Porto
R Nova da Alfândega
Auto-Estrada A1-IC1
Avenida dos Escultores
Cais do Cavaco
Via 8
Rua da Praia
Alfândega Nova Museu dos Transportes e Comunicações
Cais Capelo Ivens

Castelo do Queijo (Queijo Castle)

The name of this 17th-century fort literally means 'cheese castle', because the rocks on which it is built are thought to resemble cheese. Officially it's the fortress of St Francis Xavier. You might want to pop in for the view and the small café. ⓐ Praça de Gonçalves Zarco ⓣ 226 181 067 ⓛ 13.00–18.00 Tues–Sun ⓑ Bus: 200 ⓘ Admission charge

The Casa da Música (House of Music) hosts international performances

Igreja de São Martinho de Cedofeita (Church of Cedofeita)

Near the Rotunda da Boavista, and once the centre of a hamlet which was eventually absorbed into the city, this early-13th-century Romanesque church was built on the remains of an earlier temple and is one of the few of its type in Portugal. ⓐ Largo do Priorado ⓣ 222 005 620 ◷ 09.00–12.00, 16.00–19.30 Mon–Sat, 09.00–12.00 Sun Ⓡ Metro: A, B, C, E to Carolina Michaelis

Palácio de Cristal (Crystal Palace)

The shady park – with many pleasant walks, a pond, educational children's activities, a play area and views of Porto – was laid out in the late 19th century by architect Emile David. It was the site of a crystal palace (hence its name) designed by the British architect Thomas Dillen Jones for the international exhibition of 1865. This was pulled down, against local protests, and replaced in 1956 by the Rosa Mota pavilion, which is used for sporting, musical and other events. The pavilion also has a restaurant. The Biblioteca Municipal Almeida Garrett (public library), with free Internet access, and an art gallery are also in the grounds of the park. ⓐ Rua de Dom Manuel II (main entrance) ⓣ 225 430 360 ◷ 09.00–18.00 (Apr–Sept); 09.00–17.00 (Oct–Mar) Ⓡ Bus: 200; tram: 1E

Parque da Cidade (City Park)

The 50-hectare (124-acre) park leads straight down to the sea. It has lakes, a waterfall, lawns, woodland, a belvedere for the view, mini-golf and several activities (such as ponies for hire) that might attract children. ⓐ Avenida da Boavista ◷ Daylight hours Ⓡ Bus: 200

CULTURE

Casa Tait (Tait House)

This fine house, once British-owned, and right next to the Museu Romântico, has lovely gardens and a collection of old coins. It is also used for special events and exhibitions. ⓐ Rua Entre Quintas 219 ⓣ 226 057 000 ◷ 10.00–12.30, 14.00–17.30 Tues–Fri ⓡ Bus: 200; tram: 1E to Massarelos ⓘ Last admission 30 minutes before closing

Fundação de Serralves, Museu de Arte Contemporânea (Serralves Foundation Museum of Contemporary Art)

Just a stone's throw from the Avenida da Boavista, and the highlight, for many, of a trip to Porto: somewhere you could easily spend most of a day. The 18-hectare (45-acre) park, created by the wealthy Carlos Alberto Cabral, who lived there, was acquired by the Portuguese state in 1986; a foundation involving local companies and other organisations was set up three years later to run it. The exciting, all-white art museum, with its many angular spaces and an auditorium, was designed by Álvaro Siza Vieira, and opened in 1999. Alongside the permanent collection, with works by some big names, major themed temporary international exhibitions change every three months or so.

But there's much more to the Serralves than the works of art on display: two excellent shops with art books, design objects and gifts, a café with a terrace, which becomes a more formal restaurant in the evening, a bar, and many special events and performances through the year.

The park itself, with quirky sculptures dotted around, features a formal French garden, a wilder English one and a 'farm' with animals that children will enjoy. There is also a café in the grounds, and jazz concerts in July. Unfortunately, you can't picnic in the park.

The Art Deco **Casa de Serralves**, the luxurious pink villa of the former owners, was built between 1920 and 1940, and the superb interior, with its central gallery, impressive marble bathroom and parquet floors, is one of the finest of its type. The building now houses temporary exhibitions and other events. ⓐ Rua D João de Castro 210 ⓣ 226 156 500 ⓦ www.serralves.pt ⓛ 10.00–17.00 Tues–Fri, 10.00–20.00 Sat, Sun & public holidays (Apr–Sept);

Dig this – surreal art at the Fundação de Serralves park

10.00–17.00 Tues–Fri, 10.00–19.00 Sat, Sun & public holidays (Oct–Mar) Bus: 201, 203, 502, 504 Admission charge for park and museum or park only. Free 10.00–14.00 Sun

Museu do Carro Eléctrico (Tram Museum)
Porto was the first city in the Iberian peninsula to have a tram system, and this museum – in an old electrical power station next to the STCP tram depot by the Douro – opened in 1992. It's a fun place to go, and features trams and other vehicles dating back to the 19th century. It also has a shop and a café, and stages special events. Almeda Basílio Teles 51 226 158 185 www.museudocarroelectrico.pt 09.30–12.30, 14.30–18.00 Tues–Fri, 15.00–19.00 Sat, Sun & public holidays; open Mon by arrangement only Tram: 1E, 18 to Massarelos; bus: 1, 3, 6, 7, 14, 15, 19, 20, 36, 37, 38, 39, 41, 58, 60, 77 Admission charge

Museu Romântico (Romantic Museum)
The early-19th-century Quinta de Macieirinha, with its delightful gardens, is one of the most pleasing sights in Porto. The house was once in the countryside, but now displays the kind of interiors typically found in a wealthy 19th-century merchant's town house. It is also dedicated to Carlos Alberto, the exiled king of Piedmont-Sardinia, who died there in 1849.

Downstairs is the Solar do Vinho Porto, where you can enjoy a glass of port from a huge selection – either in the elegant lounge or on the pretty terrace, with its views of the Douro. You can get to the house either downhill via the gardens of the Palácio de Cristal or through the main entrance. Rua Entre Quintas 220 226 057 033 Museum: 10.00–12.30,

Escape from the city to the coast, at Foz do Douro

14.00–17.30 Tues–Sat, 14.00–17.30 Sun; Solar do Vinho Porto: 14.00–20.00 Mon–Thur, 14.00–24.00 Fri & Sat Bus: 200; tram: 1E to Massarelos Admission charge for museum (except Sat & Sun). Visits in small groups only. Last admission 30 minutes before closing

Museu dos Transportes e Comunicações (Transport & Communications Museum)
A little way west of Ribeira, in a huge customs house built in 1860, the collection is mainly devoted to cars – and how they work, their history, future and impact on society. Many of the intriguing exhibits are interactive. Also a good café/bar. Rua Nova da Alfândega 223 403 000 www.amtc.pt 10.00–18.00 Tues–Fri, 15.00–19.00 Sat, Sun & public holidays Tram: 1E Alfândega Admission charge

Museu do Vinho do Porto (Port Museum)
Opened in 2004, this contemporary museum (with some interactive activities for children) celebrating the history of port, is westward along the quayside from Ribeira. Housed in an 18th-century wine warehouse, it's well worth visiting for its elegantly presented displays. Rua do Monchique 45–52 222 076 300 10.00–12.30, 14.00–17.30 Tues–Sat, 14.00–17.30 Sun Tram: 1E Alfândega Admission charge

RETAIL THERAPY

There are two good shopping centres near the Rotunda da Boavista:

Centro Comercial Cidade do Porto (with four cinema screens) has food shops, a supermarket, a tobacconist, a pharmacy, perfumeries, an internet café and clothes shops such as Mango, Zara and Accessorize. ⓐ Praça do Bom Sucesso 61 ⓣ 226 006 584 ⓦ www.shoppingcidadedoporto.com ⓛ 10.00–23.00

Galeria Comercial Peninsula has mainly clothes shops, including MaxMara, Gant and Massimo Dutti. ⓐ Praça do Bom Sucesso 159 ⓣ 226 001 862 ⓛ 10.00–23.00

TAKING A BREAK

Portugalia £ ❶ Part of a national chain, this restaurant enjoys a great view over the mouth of the Douro. The menu includes good steaks and seafood and is popular with families. Alternatively, just stop for a sandwich or a drink. ⓐ Rua do Passeio Alegre ⓣ 225 321 271 ⓛ 12.00–24.00 ⓑ Bus: 200

Cafeína £–££ ❷ An atmospheric café, bar and restaurant in the Foz area with excellent creative food and a pleasant atmosphere. Fashionable and youngish, with jazz playing in the background. ⓐ Rua do Padrão 100 ⓣ 226 108 059 ⓛ 10.00–02.00 ⓑ Bus: 200, 203, 207, 500

Fundação Serralves £–££ ❸ You can visit the museum's café for either a buffet lunch or a drink (there's also a bar downstairs) or a more formal meal when it turns into a restaurant in the evening. ⓐ Rua D João de Castro 210 ⓣ 226 170 355 ⓛ Café: 12.00–19.00; restaurant: 20.00–24.00 ⓑ Bus: 201, 203, 502, 504

Shis ££ ❹ Sophisticated modern fusion cuisine at this glass-fronted place right by the Atlantic and next to a beach. High-quality specialities include sushi and seafood, and the location takes some beating, particularly when you sit out on the terrace. ⓐ Esplanada do Castelo (by Avenida do Brasil) ⓣ 226 189 593 ◷ Food served 12.00–15.00, 20.00–23.30; bar open until 03.00 Ⓝ Bus: 200

AFTER DARK

RESTAURANTS

Casa Agrícola ££ ❺ With a lively café/bar downstairs, this is an atmospheric restaurant with friendly service, providing traditional and more international dishes, such as pasta, magret of duck and roast beef. The wine list is also very impressive. If you're feeling hungry try one of their filling *açordas* (bread stews). ⓐ Rua do Bom Sucesso 241–243 ⓣ 226 053 350 ◷ Restaurant: 12.30–15.00, 20.00–22.30 Mon–Sat Ⓝ Metro: A, B, C, E to Casa da Música

Churrascão do Mar ££ ❻ One of the best fish and seafood restaurants in town, set in an impressive old house. ⓐ Rua João Grave 134–152 ⓣ 226 068 458 ◷ 12.30–15.00, 19.00–23.00 Mon–Sat Ⓝ Bus: 19, 21, 30, 78, 201

Terra ££ ❼ A stylish, lively, friendly place popular with locals, with an eclectic menu reflecting both Portuguese and Mediterranean cuisine, particularly Italian. Downstairs is a sushi bar and there is also Japanese food available upstairs.

ⓐ Rua do Padrão 103 ⓣ 226 175 171 ⓦ www.restauranteterra.com ⓛ 13.00–15.00, 19.30–02.00 (03.00 weekends) ⓑ Bus: 200, 203, 207, 500

Bull & Bear £££ ❽ In a modern building, serving celebrated creative cuisine, giving the local staples a new twist. ⓐ Avenida da Boavista 3431 ⓣ 226 107 669 ⓛ 12.30–15.00, 20.00–22.30 Mon–Fri, 20.00–22.30 Sat & Sun ⓑ Bus: 201, 502

Foz Velha £££ ❾ A local favourite for anniversaries and birthdays, with extremely high-quality modern food in a formal atmosphere. ⓐ Esplanada do Castelo 141 ⓣ 226 154 178 ⓛ 12.30–15.00, 19.30–23.00 Thur–Mon, 19.30–23.00 Wed ⓑ Bus: 200

Foz harbour

BARS & CLUBS

You'll find some of the most happening places in Porto in this area. Here are a few of them:

Bar Bazaar Not far from the Palácio de Cristal, on the river. ⓐ Cais das Pedras 13 ⓣ 226 062 113 ⓛ 16.00–02.00

New Yorker The mellow piano bar of the Sheraton hotel is a lively meeting place, particularly at weekends. And prices are reasonable for a five-star hotel. ⓐ Rua do Tenente Valadim 146 ⓣ 220 404 000 ⓛ 10.00–02.00

Pop In Foz, one of the smoothest clubs in Porto. ⓐ Rua do Padre Luís Cabral 1090 ⓣ 226 183 959 ⓛ 23.00–04.00 Thur–Sat

Trintaeum In an old building with an up-to-the-minute interior. One of the best discos in town – in the Foz area. ⓐ Rua do Passeio Alegre 564 ⓣ 226 107 567 ⓦ www.trintaeum.com (in Portuguese) ⓛ 22.30–02.00 Mon–Thur, 22.00–04.00 Fri & Sat

Triplex This restaurant (one of the better ones in Porto) and bar cover three floors of a 19th-century building. ⓐ Avenida da Boavista 911 ⓣ 226 098 968 ⓛ 12.30–03.00 Mon–Sat

Twin's A favourite for pretty party people. ⓐ Rua Passeio Alegre 1000 ⓣ 226 165 000 ⓦ www.twins.pt ⓛ 23.00–04.00

▶ *Guimarães' seven-towered castle*

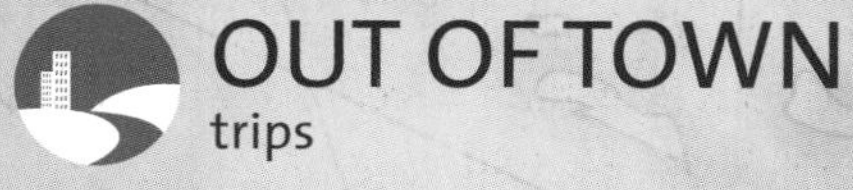

OUT OF TOWN
trips

Guimarães

'Aqui Nasceu Portugal,' says a sign on the side of a building as you walk into the centre of town: 'Portugal was born here.' And, indeed, in many ways it was, as every Portuguese schoolchild knows. The city, mostly industrial now, with textile and shoe factories among others, was the birthplace of Afonso Henriques (in 1110), the first real king of the country. It became the capital of Portucale, and a base for the defeat of the Moors and the eventual establishment of what is now Portugal. The 65,000 people who live here are proud of its past and looking forward to its future; the old town centre was put on the UNESCO World Heritage List in 2001, and the city was nominated as a European Capital of Culture for 2012. Those accolades, along with the Euro 2004 football championships (Guimarães has an important club and ground), have led to a considerable improvement of the local infrastructure, tourist facilities and travel connections.

The town was founded in the tenth century, when the local monastery attracted a settlement and the castle was built for its defence. Rua de Santa Maria evolved to link the two. Because of the monastery, which grew in importance, the town also became a centre of pilgrimage, and walls were erected to protect it (though they were mostly pulled down in the 19th century). The layout of the town centre today is much as it was in the 15th century; most of the buildings you'll see when you wander around the highly attractive historic centre date from the 17th century. Guimarães was granted the status of a city in 1853; it is also home to a major university. The main event, the Festas de Cidade e Gualterianas on the first weekend of August, dates

The pretty houses of Guimarães

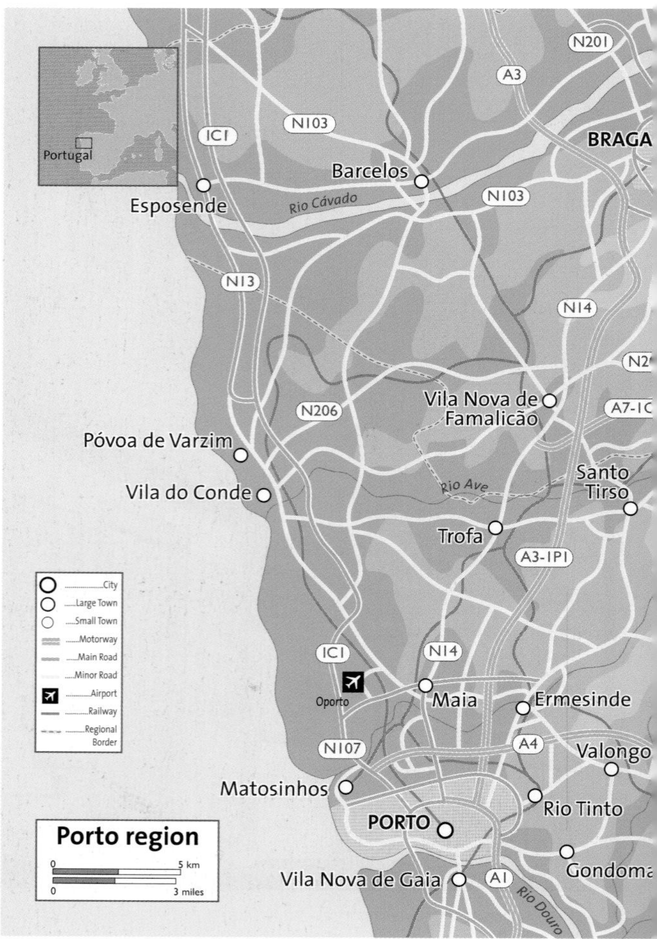
Porto region
0
5 km
0
3 miles
Portugal
City
Large Town
Small Town
Motorway
Main Road
Minor Road
Airport
Railway
Regional Border
N201
A3
N103
IC1
BRAGA
Barcelos
Esposende
Rio Cávado
N103
N13
N14
N2
Vila Nova de Famalicão
A7-IC
N206
Póvoa de Varzim
Vila do Conde
Rio Ave
Santo Tirso
Trofa
A3-IP1
IC1
N14
Oporto
Maia
Ermesinde
N107
A4
Valongo
Matosinhos
Rio Tinto
PORTO
Gondoma
Vila Nova de Gaia
A1
Rio Douro

N103
Serra da Cabreira
Póvoa de Lanhoso
N
Cabeceiras de Basto
BRAGA
A11
Guimarães
Fafe
617m
Penha
Rio Tâmega
Celorico de Basto
Mondim de Basto
N101
Vizela
Felgueiras
PORTUGAL
Lixa
N15
IP9
Lousada
Amarante
IP4
Paços de Ferreira
A4
Rio Sousa
N101
aredes
Penafiel
Marco de Canaveses
Baião
Serra do Mardo
PORTO
Resende
Rio Douro

back to 1452. There is also a classical music festival in late May and June, and the important Jazz Festival in November.

GETTING THERE

Guimarães, in the Minho province, is around 60 km (37 miles) northeast from central Porto. The best way to get there from Porto is by train from S Bento or Campanhã stations; fares are modest, and the journey takes a little over an hour in clean, punctual trains. You can also drive via the A3 or go by bus (a number of bus companies operating in Porto go there), but the bus can take two hours. You can park outside the UNESCO area at the railway station and the Vila Flor nearby. The bus station is to the southwest of the city centre, about 15 minutes' walk. The train station is also to the south, a short walk from the historic centre.

The main tourist office is **Posto de Turismo da Alameda** (ⓐ Alameda de S Dâmaso 83 ⓣ 253 412 450 ⓛ 09.30–12.30, 14.00–18.30 Mon–Fri). **Posto de Turismo** (ⓐ Praça de Santiago 37 ⓣ 253 518 790 ⓛ 09.30–18.30 Mon–Fri, 10.00–18.00 Sat & public holidays, 10.00–13.00 Sun) is in the old town. The tourism website is ⓦ www.guimaraesturismo.com

You can hire an MP3 audio-guide in English about the old town from the Posto de Turismo.

SIGHTS & ATTRACTIONS

The primary attraction is the mainly pedestrianised historic centre and its atmospheric cobbled streets and squares, with their pretty houses. The squares – Largo da Oliveira, Praça de Santiago and Largo João Franco – all have several enticing cafés. You'll notice that none of the houses has a TV aerial or satellite dish – the result of local incentives to preserve the look of the place. The city has also bought a number of buildings in the old town and put them to new use to ensure their future. As a result there is a pleasing coherence to Guimarães, with a real sense of the past. You should easily be able to get around it in half a day, but allow a full day if you want to visit all the museums. The gardens by the castle and the ducal palace are a very pleasant place to take a break. As you walk around you'll see five small early-18th-century shrines with sculptures depicting the Stations of the Cross, a testament to the devotion of the local population.

Antigos Paços do Concelho (Old Council Chamber)
The Old Council Chamber, dating from the 14th century, but remodelled at the beginning of the 17th century, has a painted wooden ceiling, and is above the arches between Praça de Santiago and the Largo da Oliveira. It now houses the Museu de Arte Primitiva Moderna – a museum of naïve art of varying quality. ⓐ Largo da Oliveira ⓣ 253 414 186 ⓛ 09.00–12.30, 14.00–17.30 Mon–Fri

Capela de São Miguel (Chapel of St Michael)
Between the castle and the ducal palace, this small, simple Romanesque chapel was built in the early 12th century. It is thought to be where Afonso Henriques was baptised and contains the tombs of several of his knights. ⓐ Rua de Santa Maria ⓣ 253 412 273 ⓛ 10.00–18.00 Tues–Sun

Castelo (Castle)

After the original monastery was established on the orders of the Countess Mumadona Dias, the castle was built in the 10th century to fend off attacks by Moors and Normans. It was strengthened in the 12th century and was enlarged in later centuries. According to tradition, King Afonso Henriques was born here. When the castle lost its defensive purpose, it became a prison, and was subsequently abandoned and fell into decline until the 1940s when it was finally declared a National Monument and restored. After admiring the castle, climb to the top of the battlements to get a view of Guimarães and the surrounding countryside – and if you go through the small opening to get to the top of the keep (❶ Admission charge), there's an even better view. ⓐ Rua de Santa Maria ⓣ 253 412 273 ⓛ 10.00–18.00 Tues–Sun (main tower closed at lunchtime)

Igreja de Nossa Senhora da Oliveira (Church of Our Lady of the Olive Tree)

In the heart of the old town, this church was rebuilt on the orders of João I at the end of the 14th century. The tower was added in 1513, and the chancel enlarged at the end of the 17th century. The chapel in the sacristy is covered in tiles. Next to the church is the Salado memorial, a Gothic monument dating from the 14th century, built to commemorate the battle of Salado in 1340. ⓐ Largo da Oliveira ⓛ 08.30–12.00, 15.30–19.30 Mon–Sat, 09.00–13.00, 17.00–20.00 Sun

Penha

The hill of Penha is 2 km (1 mile) to the southeast of Guimarães. You can get up the wooded slopes to the 617-m (2,020-ft) peak

Pick a café and watch the world go by on Largo da Oliveira

by car, bus (from opposite the main tourist office) or, by far the most fun option, the ten-minute cable-car ride from the Parque das Hortas. Either way, you will find a campsite, a mini-golf course, walks, jogging circuits, horse riding, picnic areas and restaurants and cafés on the hill. You'll also get superb views of the surrounding area. The main sight (on the lower slopes) is the Mosteiro de Santa Marinha da Costa, founded in 1154, probably on the site of a pre-Roman temple. The monastery was originally Augustinian, but from 1528 housed monks of the Order of St Jerome. The 18th-century church has a rococo façade, with mid-19th-century alterations in the interior. The monastery was badly damaged by a fire in 1951, but was sensitively restored, and is now a *pousada* (state-run hotel), with the gardens and some areas open to the public.

Praça de Santiago (Santiago Square)

Originally medieval, the square, with its lively café terraces in good weather, is named after St James. He was supposed to have brought an image of the Virgin Mary to place in a pagan temple that once stood in the square, where most of the houses are 17th century.

CULTURE

Centro Cultural Vila Flor (Vila Flor Cultural Centre)

This modern centre – near the railway station and on the way to the old town – opened in 2005 in the grounds of a 17th-century mansion, as part of the city's attempts to prepare for the 2012 European Capital of Culture nomination. It has exhibition spaces, parking, two state-of-the-art auditoriums, and is now the base for the Jazz Festival. It also has a lively and stylish café on the lower level (until 02.00 on most days, 04.00 during the Jazz Festival). The old Vila Flor houses temporary art exhibitions. There are performances, exhibitions and events throughout the year, and it's well worth checking out what's on. The terraced gardens are also very appealing. Avenida D Afonso Henriques 701 253 424 700 www.aoficina.pt Vary according to events, but 08.00–12.00, 14.00–16.00 for gardens Admission charge for events and exhibitions

Museu de Alberto Sampaio (Alberto Sampaio Museum)

This museum – occupying an old priory, chapter house and cloister – was created in 1928 on the site of the monastery around which Guimarães originally grew up. It houses the treasures of the local churches. Some of the exhibits go back to medieval times and there is a fine collection of silverware. For a museum of mostly religious artefacts, it is remarkably interesting and the high-quality exhibits are well displayed. Rua Alfredo Guimarães 253 423 910 10.00–18.00 Tues–Sun Admission charge (free Sun mornings)

Museu Arqueológico Martins Sarmento (Martins Sarmento Archaeological Museum)

Outside the old town, near Largo do Toural, the city's main square, this archaeological museum is housed in an 18th–19th-century mansion with a splendid garden, once owned by the archaeologist after whom it was named. The expertly displayed exhibits are of the pre-Roman culture of the area. Rua Paio Galvão

ⓣ 253 415 969 ⓛ 09.30–12.30, 14.00–18.00 Tues–Sun
ⓘ Admission charge

Paço dos Duques (Ducal Palace)
This massive palace was built in the 15th century, for Afonso, later Duke of Bragança, illegitimate son of King João I. The style is unusual for Portugal – the steep roofs and cylindrical chimneys are more reminiscent of northern Europe – since the architect was probably French. The palace went into serious decline from the 16th century and was near ruin by the 20th century, but was rebuilt between 1937 and 1959, and then became a museum. Attracting 300,000 visitors a year, it is now the third most visited attraction in Portugal, as well as being the president's official northern residence. The collection consists of tapestries, furniture, porcelain and other decorative art from the 17th and 18th centuries, as well as arms and armour from the 15th and 16th centuries. Concerts and other events are also held here. The Renaissance fountain in Largo Martins Sarmento, near the palace, was built in 1583 and originally stood in Toural, the city's main square. ⓐ Rua de Santa Maria ⓣ 253 412 273 ⓛ 10.00–18.00 Tues–Sun ⓘ Admission charge (free Sun mornings)

RETAIL THERAPY

There aren't a huge number of shopping opportunities in the old town, but there are a couple of good craft shops selling pottery, embroidery and wooden objects:
Art'iago ⓐ Praça de Santiago ⓣ 253 415 795 ⓛ Varies seasonally
Prometeu ⓐ Rua de Santa Maria ⓣ 253 512 640 ⓛ Varies seasonally

The imposing form of the Paço dos Duques (Ducal Palace)

TAKING A BREAK

Cinecitta £ Sit under the arches (if it rains) or outside in the square at this snack bar with movie posters on the walls. You can get salads, sandwiches, soups and ice cream. ⓐ Praça de Santiago 26 ⓛ 08.00–24.00 Tues & Sun, 08.00–02.00 Wed–Sat

Cozinha Regional Santiago £–££ A comforting place serving good fish, veal, sausages and daily specials. Tables outside in good weather. ⓐ Praça de Santiago 16–17 ⓣ 253 516 669 ⓛ 12.00–15.00, 19.00–22.00 Mon–Sat

El Rei £–££ Well located, and considered by many to be the best restaurant in the old town. ⓐ Praça de Santiago 20 ⓣ 253 419 096 ⓛ 13.00–15.00, 19.30–22.00 Mon–Sat

Solar do Arco ££ A local favourite, serving regional cuisine and daily specials. ⓐ Rua de Santa Maria 50 ⓣ 253 513 072 ⓛ 10.00–24.00 daily (Mar–Dec); 10.00–24.00 Wed–Mon (Jan–Feb)

ACCOMMODATION

Guimarães Youth Hostel £ The budget option in town, the youth hostel has accommodation options ranging from a self-catering apartment to double bedrooms and dorms, plus the usual kitchen and bar. Disabled access. ⓐ Complexo Multifuncional de Couros – Largo da Cidade ⓣ 253 421 380 ⓦ www.pousadasjuventude.pt

Hotel Ibis Guimarães ££ With 67 comfortable rooms, the Ibis offers a good value and reliable choice in the centre of town. Avenida Conde Margaride 12, Creixomil 253 424 900 www.ibishotel.com

Pousada da Oliveira ££ With a very good restaurant, in a row of 16th-century houses. Both comfortable and tastefully decorated. Rua de Santa Maria 253 514 157 www.pousadas.pt

Largo do Toural is the main square in Guimarães

Braga

Braga has been one of the main centres of Catholicism in Portugal since its development in the late 11th century under its first bishop. Founded as the Roman settlement of Bracara Augusta (probably of earlier Celtic origin), the town grew around its cathedral and was eventually walled. It remained a devout backwater until the 16th century, when the bishop Diogo de Sousa developed it further and fine Renaissance architecture was added. The historic town centre remained largely unchanged until the 19th century, apart from a flourish of Baroque buildings a century earlier. Many of the greatest changes took place only after the Revolution of 1974, so that Braga is now the third largest city in Portugal, with a population of 150,000, plus thousands of university students. It is a centre of the textile industry. The centre, which was seriously deteriorating, was comprehensively restored from the 1980s onwards. Braga's reputation as a pretty conservative place is offset by the student population, which ensures that it's far livelier these days. The city also has an impressive football stadium, built with one side against a cliff for Euro 2004. Indeed, in the words of one resident, the main activities of Braga today are 'praying, shopping and construction'. The most important festivals are São João in June, Bom Jesus (at Whitsun) and Semana Santa (Holy Week, before Easter) – all of them lively and colourful.

GETTING THERE

Braga is 53 km (33 miles) northeast of Porto. You can get there by train from S Bento or Campanhã stations in only an hour (the best and most reliable option) or you can drive or take a Renex bus, both of which will take over an hour. From Guimarães, it's only a 30-minute drive or 45-minute bus ride to Braga, and it's well worth combining the two for a day trip. The bus station is a short walk to the west of the town centre, and the modern railway station (which retains the exterior of the old, blue-tiled one) a slightly longer walk to the south. There are several car parks, a number of them underground.

Tourist office ⓐ Avenida da Liberdade 1 ⓣ 253 262 550 ⓦ www.cm-braga.pt ⓛ 09.00–19.00 Mon–Fri, 09.00–12.30, 14.00–17.30 Sat & Sun (June–Sept); 09.00–12.30, 14.00–18.30 Mon–Fri, 09.00–12.30, 14.00–17.30 Sat & Sun (Oct–May)

SIGHTS & ATTRACTIONS

There aren't that many formal sights in Braga, and you'll probably want to simply wander round the uplifting, surprisingly broad and mainly pedestrianised streets of the old town, the large and lively main square, the **Praça da República**, with its fountains and cafés, and the shops of the recently part-pedestrianised Avenida da Liberdade which comes off it. Down the avenue, have a look at the old theatre (Teatro Circo), sumptuously restored inside: it reopened in 2006 after a closure of seven years. The tower you see behind the Praça da República is the Torre de Menagem, the keep of a castle built in 1738. The old town is just south of the Praça da República. The first street to head for in the old town should be Rua do Souto. Note, as you walk around, that many of the shops sell religious objects. At the café called **Frigideiras do Cantinho** (ⓐ Largo S João do Souto 1) check out the Roman

remains below the glass floor. If you have time, also try to get to Bom Jesus (see below). You should be able to see the best of Braga and Bom Jesus in little more than half a day.

Antigo Paço Arquiepiscopal (Old Archbishop's Palace)
The massive old bishop's palace, near the cathedral, consists of three buildings dating from different periods. The east wing, facing the attractive Santa Bárbara gardens, is 16th century but in the Gothic style; the west wing is late-18th-century Baroque, and the south part of the edifice is a mixture of styles from the 16th to 18th centuries. The building now houses the municipal library, as well as being part of the University of Minho. Admire the fine reading room with its coffered ceiling. ⓐ Rua da Misericórdia or Largo do Paço ⓣ 253 601 187 ⓛ 09.00–12.00, 14.00–20.00 Mon–Fri

Bom Jesus do Monte
Try not to miss this church and its esplanade, a major attraction of the region and one of the most famous buildings in Portugal. It's on the top of a hill 5 km (3 miles) east of the city centre and you can reach it by climbing the 800 steps (with 19 chapels on the way up) of the magnificent stairway as pilgrims do. Alternatively, go by bus and foot (take the No 2 from Avenida da Liberdade) or get to the top by a water-powered late-19th-century funicular, which climbs 115 m (381 ft). Otherwise you can drive or take a reasonably priced taxi. When you get to the top of the hill, with its panoramic views, you will find the amazing Baroque church commissioned by Archbishop Maura-Teles in 1723, completed 60 years later, with a double staircase leading up

The church of Bom Jesus do Monte, one of the most famous in Portugal

to it – a local favourite for weddings. Bom Jesus more or less turns into a resort area in summer and at weekends, with people bringing picnics to eat in the gardens, eating at the hotels and cafés by the church or taking part in the various activities available. ⓐ Bom Jesus do Monte, Tenões ⓣ 253 676 636 Ⓛ 08.30–18.30 (May–Sept), 08.30–17.30 (Oct–Apr)

Sé Catedral (Cathedral)

The magnificent cathedral is the oldest in Portugal, consecrated in 1093 on the site of a Moorish mosque. The building is essentially Romanesque and Gothic, with Baroque alterations. There are several chapels, and you will see many people praying at shrines. Note the two Baroque organs and the tiles in the main chapel. Try also to visit the treasury upstairs (guided tour only), one of the richest in Portugal, and the Capela dos Reis (Kings' Chapel) with its Gothic vaulted roof. ⓐ Rua D Paio Mendes ⓣ 253 263 317 Ⓛ Church: 07.45–19.00 (Apr–Sept), 07.45–18.30 (Oct–Mar); treasury: 08.30–17.30 ❶ Admission charge for treasury

CULTURE

Museu da Imagem (Photographic Museum)

Braga's photographic museum, opened in 1999, is in an old deep-pink house, just by the Arco da Porta Nova, the city gate dating from 1772. Check the tourist office website for details of the latest exhibitions. ⓐ Campo das Hortas 35–37 ⓣ 253 278 633 Ⓛ 11.00–19.00 Tues–Fri, 14.30–18.00 Sat & Sun ❶ Admission charge

The striking scarlet façade of the Photographic Museum

Palácio dos Biscainhos (Biscainhos Palace)
An 18th-century Baroque palace, with fine gardens, which has a collection of decorative arts, redolent of the lifestyles of 17th- and 18th-century aristocrats, and completely in keeping with the building. ⓐ Rua dos Biscainhos ⓣ 253 217 645 ◷ 10.00–12.15, 14.00–17.30 Tues–Sun ❗ Admission charge

RETAIL THERAPY

You'll find several craft, clothes and shoe shops in the old town as well as chain, designer and international shops in the Avenida da Liberdade.

TAKING A BREAK

A Brasileira £ A blue-tiled exterior in this old-fashioned but charming café, which is something of a local institution. ⓐ Largo Barão de São Martinho ⓣ 253 262 104 ◷ 08.00–24.00

Café Astoria £ One of the city's best (and oldest) cafés, with good snacks and a pleasant atmosphere. ⓐ Praça da República ⓣ 253 273 944 ◷ 09.00–02.00

Café Vianna £ Great snacks in this fashionable Art-Nouveau place. ⓐ Praça da República ⓣ 253 262 336 ◷ 08.00–02.00

Abade de Priscos £–££ A reliable restaurant serving Portuguese specialities. ⓐ Praça Mouzinho de Albuquerque 7 ⓣ 253 276 650 ◷ 20.00–23.00 Mon, 12.00–15.00, 20.00–23.00 Tues–Sat

The Praça da República is a good place to start your visit

Brito's £–££ Good traditional food and local wine in a friendly setting. ⓐ Praça Mouzinho de Albuquerque 49 ⓣ 253 617 576 ⓛ 09.30–late Thur–Tues

Inácio ££ High-quality local cooking in a traditional atmosphere. ⓐ Campo das Hortas 4 ⓣ 253 613 3 25 ⓛ 12.00–15.00, 19.00–22.00 Wed–Mon

The elegant interior of Porto's São Bento station

PRACTICAL
information

Directory

GETTING THERE

By air

Porto's international airport, Francisco Sá Carneiro, is served by a number of direct flights from the UK. TAP Air Portugal (the national carrier) provides the only scheduled service. Low-cost airline easyJet, which recently started to fly to Porto, is the best all-round bet for price and flight times, and the airport is also served by Ryanair. Between them these airlines provide regular flights from Bristol, Birmingham, Liverpool, London Gatwick, London Heathrow and London Stansted.

easyJet ⓦ www.easyjet.com

TAP Air Portugal ⓣ Reservations: 0845 601 0932

ⓦ www.flytap.com

Ryanair ⓦ www.ryanair.com

Many people are aware that air travel emits CO_2, which contributes to climate change. You may be interested in the possibility of lessening the environmental impact of your flight through the charity **Climate Care**, which offsets your CO_2 by funding environmental projects around the world. Visit ⓦ www.jpmorganclimatecare.com

By rail

You can get to Porto's Campanhã station by train from the UK via Eurostar to Paris, onward through France via Bordeaux and then through Spain and northern Portugal, changing trains at least twice more – a long and complex journey that will probably be more expensive than flying.

Rail Europe ⓣ 08705 848 848 ⓦ www.raileurope.co.uk
CP (Portuguese Railways) ⓦ www.cp.pt

The easiest way to plan your journey is to consult the monthly *Thomas Cook European Rail Timetable* (ⓦ www.thomascookpublishing.com).

By road

You'll need at least one overnight stop if you drive from the UK to Porto (via France and Spain), crossing the Channel to France by Eurotunnel or ferry, but if you don't want such a long drive, take a ferry overnight to northern Spain (Santander or Bilbao). It will still take the best part of a day to drive to Porto, and costs can be high.
Eurotunnel ⓣ 08705 35 35 35 ⓦ www.eurotunnel.com
Brittany Ferries ⓦ www.brittany-ferries.com
P&O Ferries ⓦ www.poferries.com
ACP (Portuguese Automobile Club) for emergency assistance ⓣ 228 340 001
Route planner ⓦ www.rac.co.uk or www.theaa.com

TRAVEL INSURANCE

Visitors from the UK are covered by EU reciprocal health schemes while in Portugal; you will need a European Health Insurance Card (EHIC). This guarantees emergency treatment only. Always make sure you have adequate travel insurance, covering not only health, but possessions, etc. All non-EU travellers should make sure they have adequate insurance before they travel.

ENTRY FORMALITIES

Passports are needed by UK visitors and all others, except EU citizens who can produce a national identity card. EU (including UK) citizens do not require a visa. US, Canadian, Australian and New Zealand visitors do not require a visa for visits of up to three months. Other travellers should check in their own country about visa requirements. Ⓦ www.eurovisa.info

Residents of the UK, Ireland and other EU countries may bring into Portugal personal possessions and goods for personal use, including a reasonable amount of tobacco and alcohol, provided they have been bought in the EU. The same applies to taking alcohol and tobacco back home. There are few formalities at the points of entry into Portugal. Residents of non-EU countries, and EU residents arriving from a non-EU country, may bring in up to 200 cigarettes or 50 cigars or 250 g (9 oz) of tobacco; 4 litres (5 bottles) of wine; and 1 litre of spirits and liqueurs.

MONEY

The euro (€) (€1 = 100 cents) comes in notes of €5, €10, €20, €50, €100, €200 and €500, and coins of €1 and €2 and 1, 2, 5, 10, 20 and 50 cents.

Multibanco (ATM machines) can be found at the airport, and are widely available around Porto. They accept most debit and credit cards. They are the quickest and most convenient (and often the cheapest) way to obtain cash. Instructions are normally available in English.

Credit cards (especially Visa and MasterCard) are generally accepted except at smaller shops, in simple restaurants and at markets. There are plenty of banks and bureaux de change.

HEALTH, SAFETY & CRIME

It is safe to drink tap water, as most people do, although some prefer instead to drink mineral water, which is cheap. There are no major precautions you need to take when eating local food – except perhaps being careful with seafood. On the whole, however, you need worry no more than at home.

Medical care in Portugal is of a decent standard, but expensive unless you have suitable travel insurance. Most minor ailments can be dealt with at *farmácias* (pharmacies), indicated by green cross signs, where qualified staff offer medical advice and dispense a wide range of medicines.

Porto is generally safe, but you should be careful late at night in the alleys near the river and in or near the railway station. Otherwise, take the usual sensible precautions against pickpockets and bag-snatchers, keeping your bag or camera close to you.

In general the police try to be helpful, but they may not speak English and can be somewhat authoritarian: try not to argue. There are three main types of police: municipal police (Polícia Municipal) are unarmed and largely deal with traffic; PSP (Polícia de Segurança Pública) wear blue uniforms and deal with crime and lost property; GNR (Guarda Nacional Republicana) wear blue-grey uniforms and operate in country districts and on motorways. Special tourist police units also patrol areas such as Ribeira.

If you are robbed, make a statement at your nearest police station. This will greatly help when making an insurance claim and may often be essential.

See also Emergencies (page 136).

OPENING HOURS

Some shops are open 09.00 or 10.00 to 18.00 or 19.00 Monday to Saturday, while others take a lunchtime break and open 09.00–13.00 and 15.00–19.00. Many shops are closed on Saturday afternoon. Large supermarkets and shopping centres open seven days a week. The covered Bolhão market in Porto is open 08.00–17.00 Monday to Friday and 08.00–13.00 Saturday.

Offices usually open 09.00–13.00 and 15.00–17.00 Monday to Friday; banks open 08.30–15.00 Monday to Friday. All are closed on public holidays.

Museums, galleries and monuments normally open 10.00–12:30 and 14.00–18.00, although some don't close for lunch. Many also close on public holidays, and almost all on Monday or Wednesday (if they are palaces). Some churches close for a couple of hours during the day; others are kept locked and you will have to approach the caretaker to be let in.

Pharmacies are open 09.00–13.00 and 15.00–19.00 Monday to Saturday (some closing Saturday afternoon, others opening Sunday). You will find a list of late or 24-hour pharmacies on the door or window of those which keep regular hours.

TOILETS

Public toilets aren't particularly widespread, though you will find them at the railway station, and there are coin-operated cubicles in some of Porto's main squares. The best bet is to use those at shopping centres, museums and monuments, which tend to be well kept. Otherwise, having a drink at one of the smarter hotels or cafés is also a good option. But beware of simpler bars and eating places, where facilities might easily be insalubrious.

CHILDREN

The Portuguese, like most southern Europeans, are highly welcoming towards children. The majority of hotels will normally be very helpful if you are travelling with small children and most restaurants will gladly serve them. Remember though that servings are large, so ask for a *meia dose* (half-portion).

Sun protection will be required only in the summer. Insect bites, however, might be a problem, and you should bring sting-relief and other items with you – or you will find them on sale in pharmacies.

Special infant needs, such as baby food and nappies, are widely available from supermarkets and other outlets, but for a shorter stay it is easier to bring familiar brands from home. Don't expect much in the way of nappy-changing facilities.

A Ribeira farmácia *(pharmacy)*

Infants (under 5) are allowed in free to museums and other attractions, and under-12s pay half price. The same applies to trains, but not the metro, trams and buses – where you will have to pay full fare for them.

Unfortunately very few of Porto's attractions are aimed at young children, but a trip up the Douro might be a good idea, as might a tram ride (and the Tram Museum). The area at the mouth of the Douro is pleasant to visit, as are the Parque de Serralves and the Parque da Cidade (see page 91). The garden of Palácio de Cristal (see page 91) has a play area and a building with various computer activities for children. Also worth bearing in mind is Children's Week in May (see page 9).

COMMUNICATIONS

Internet

Internet access is widespread in Porto, with Internet cafés and connections fairly easy to find, including at bigger post offices and in libraries, and all the larger or smarter hotels provide Internet connections. Wi-Fi coverage is also good. Check for your nearest Internet point with your hotel or the local tourist office. Expect to pay around €2–3 per hour.

Phone

Card- and (rarer) coin-operated public phone booths are widely available. Some of Porto's phone booths are based on the old red British type. You can buy *cartões telefónicos* (phone cards) at newsagents, tobacconists, post offices and kiosks – cards come at various prices; PIN-activated cards are cheaper for long distance and international calls; some phones accept credit cards.

TELEPHONING PORTUGAL

Telephone numbers in Porto start with 22, followed by seven digits. When calling from anywhere in Portugal (including Porto), dial all nine digits. To call Porto from outside Portugal, dial the international prefix (00) followed by 351 (the country code for Portugal), then the nine-digit number.

TELEPHONING ABROAD

To call abroad from Portugal dial 00, followed by the country code (UK 44, Republic of Ireland 353, USA and Canada 1, Australia 61, New Zealand 64, South Africa 27), the area code (leaving out the first 0 if there is one) and the number.

The cheapest time for calls is 21.00–09.00 Monday to Friday, and all day at weekends and on public holidays. Incidentally, if you buy a Porto Card at a tourist office (see page 135), it will come with a free phone card with €1.50 credit.

Porto has good mobile-phone coverage, but check with your service provider before you leave home which local service you should use to get the best rates.

Useful numbers include local directory enquiries ⓣ 118; international directory enquiries ⓣ 177; international operator ⓣ 171 (reverse charge calls). Freephone numbers start with 800 and Portuguese mobile numbers start with 9.

Post

Post offices (marked CCT) can be found throughout Porto. The **main post office** (ⓐ Praça General Humberto Delgado

(t) 223 400 200) is open 08.00–21.00 Monday to Friday, 09.00–18.00 Saturday and 09.00–12.30, 14.00–18.00 Sunday; smaller offices open 09.00–18.00 Monday to Friday. All post offices are closed on public holidays. You can buy stamps (*selos*) at post offices or at tobacconists. Postcards to the UK and Ireland take around a week but somewhat longer to non-European destinations. Regular postboxes are red (the blue ones are for special deliveries and airmail) and resemble those found in Britain.

ELECTRICITY

Portugal runs on 220 V with two-pin plugs. British appliances will need a simple adaptor, best obtained in most UK electrical shops or at the Eurostar station or the airport you leave from. You might have difficulty finding adaptors in Porto. US and other equipment designed for 110 V will normally need a transformer.

TRAVELLERS WITH DISABILITIES

Portugal isn't generally well adapted to the needs of travellers with disabilities, and Porto's steep hills and cobbled streets aren't particularly easy to navigate. There are good facilities for those with disabilities at the airport, in some museums and the more modern hotels, as well as at many metro stations (some have lifts) and on newer local trains. Otherwise, although things are improving all the time, you might find the city and its attractions difficult to access. Check with the tourist office (see opposite) for more information.

Secretariado Nacional para a Reabilitação e Integração das Pessoas com Deficiência National government organisation providing information about accessibility. Ⓐ Avenida Conde de Valbom 63, Lisbon Ⓣ 217 929 500

RADAR The principal UK forum and pressure group for people with disabilities. Ⓐ 12 City Forum, 250 City Road, London EC1V 8AF Ⓣ 020 7250 3222 Ⓦ www.radar.org.uk

SATH (Society for Accessible Travel & Hospitality) advises US-based travellers with disabilities. Ⓐ 347 Fifth Ave, Suite 610, New York, NY 10016 Ⓣ 212 447 7284 Ⓦ www.sath.org

TOURIST INFORMATION

There are three tourist offices (*Turismo*) in the middle of Porto:

The main city one: Ⓐ Rua Clube dos Fenianos 25 Ⓣ 223 393 472 Ⓦ www.portoturismo.pt Ⓛ 09.00–17.30 daily (mid-Sept–mid-July); 09.00–19.00 daily (mid-July–mid-Sept)

In the UNESCO World Heritage area: Ⓐ Rua do Infante D Henrique 63 Ⓣ 222 060 412/413 Ⓦ www.portoturismo.pt Ⓛ 09.00–17.30 daily (mid-Sept–mid-July); 09.00–19.00 daily (mid-July–mid-Sept). Closed public holidays

The state tourist office (ITP): Ⓐ Praça Dom João I 43 Ⓣ 222 057 514 Ⓛ 09.00–19.30 Mon–Fri, 09.30–15.30 Sat, Sun & public holidays

Portuguese national tourist website Ⓦ www.visitportugal.com

Regional website Ⓦ www.visitportoandnorth.com

Online directory Ⓦ www.portugalvirtual.pt, with much useful information

Emergencies

For all emergency services (national number) ⓣ 112

MEDICAL SERVICES

The main hospitals are:

Hospital Geral de Santo António Some English-speaking doctors. ⓐ Largo Prof Abel Salazar ⓣ 222 077 500

Hospital Escolar São João To the north of the city. ⓐ Alameda Prof Hernâni Monteiro ⓣ 225 512 100

Ask your hotel, the consulate or the tourist office for a list of English-speaking doctors and dentists near where you are staying.

POLICE

The main stations are:

Polícia de Turismo (Tourist Police) English spoken, near the main tourist office, and the best place to go, if you can. ⓐ Rua Clube dos Fenianos 11 ⓣ 222 081 833 ⓛ 08.00–02.00

Polícia de Segurança Pública ⓐ Rua Augousto Rosa ⓣ 222 087 848

Polícia Municipal ⓐ Bairro Rainha D Leonor ⓣ 226 198 260

EMBASSIES & CONSULATES

Australian Embassy ⓐ 2nd floor, Avenida da Liberdade 200, 1250-147 Lisbon ⓣ 213 101 500 ⓛ 09.00–17.00 Mon–Fri

Canadian Embassy ⓐ 3rd floor, Avenida da Liberdade 196, 1269-121 Lisbon ⓣ 213 164 600 ⓛ 13.30–16.30 Mon–Fri

EMERGENCY PHRASES

Help!	**Fire!**	**Stop!**
Socorro!	Fogo!	Pare!
Sookohrroo!	*Fohgoo!*	*Pahreh!*

Call an ambulance/a doctor/the police/the fire brigade!
Chame uma ambulância/um médico/a polícia/ os bombeiros!
Shami ooma amboolangsya/oong mehdeekoo/ a pooleesseeya/oosh bombehroosh!

Irish Embassy Ⓐ Rua da Imprensa à Estrela 1–4, 1200-684 Lisbon Ⓣ 213 929 440 Ⓛ 09.30–12.30 Mon–Fri
South African Consulate Ⓐ Rua António José da Costa 78, 4150-090 Porto Ⓣ 226 076 010 Ⓛ 09.00–12.00 Mon–Fri
UK Consulate Ⓐ Travessa Barão de Forrester 86, 4400-034 Porto (Vila Nova de Gaia) Ⓣ 226 184 789 Ⓛ 09.30–12.30, 14.30–16.00 Mon–Fri
US Consulate Ⓐ Avenida da Boavista 3523, 4100-139 Porto Ⓣ 226 186 607 Ⓛ 08.00–12.00, 13.00–17.00 Mon–Fri

ACKNOWLEDGEMENTS

Thomas Cook Publishing wishes to thank ANWER BATI, to whom the copyright belongs, for the photographs in this book, except for the following images:

Cristovao/Dreamstime.com, page 101; Jordi Cubells Biela/Fotolia.com, page 30; Rui Saraiva/BigStockPhoto.com, page 115; TAOLMOR/Fotolia.com, pages 40–41; Martyn Vickery/Alamy, page 125.

For CAMBRIDGE PUBLISHING MANAGEMENT LIMITED:
Project editor: Kate Taylor
Copy editor: Paul Hines
Layout: Paul Queripel
Proofreaders: Michele Greenbank & Cath Senker

Send your thoughts to
books@thomascook.com

- **Found a great bar, club, shop or must-see sight that we don't feature?**
- **Like to tip us off about any information that needs a little updating?**
- **Want to tell us what you love about this handy little guidebook and more importantly how we can make it even handier?**

Then here's your chance to tell all! Send us ideas, discoveries and recommendations today and then look out for your valuable input in the next edition of this title.

Email the above address (stating the title) or write to:
pocket guides Series Editor, Thomas Cook Publishing, PO Box 227, Coningsby Road, Peterborough PE3 8SB, UK.

WHAT'S IN YOUR GUIDEBOOK?

Independent authors Impartial up-to-date information from our travel experts who meticulously source local knowledge.

Experience Thomas Cook's 165 years in the travel industry and guidebook publishing enriches every word with expertise you can trust.

Travel know-how Thomas Cook has thousands of staff working around the globe, all living and breathing travel.

Editors Travel-publishing professionals, pulling everything together to craft a perfect blend of words, pictures, maps and design.

You, the traveller We deliver a practical, no-nonsense approach to information, geared to how you really use it.

Useful phrases

English	Portuguese	*Approx pronunciation*
BASICS		
Yes	Sim	*Seem*
No	Não	*Nown*
Please	Por favor	*Poor favohr*
Thank you	Obrigado/a	*Ohbreegahdoo/a*
Hello	Olá	*Ohlah*
Goodbye	Adeus	*Adayoosh*
Excuse me	Com licença	*Cong lisensah*
Sorry	Desculpe	*Dishkoolper*
That's okay	Está bem	*Istah bayng*
Do you speak English?	Fala Inglês?	*Fahla eenglaysh?*
Good morning	Bom día	*Bohm deea*
Good afternoon	Boa tarde	*Boha tahrd*
Good evening	Boa noite	*Boha noyt*
Goodnight	Boa noite	*Boha noyt*
My name is ...	Chamo-me ...	*Shamoo-mi ...*
NUMBERS		
One	Um	*Oong*
Two	Dois	*Doysh*
Three	Três	*Traysh*
Four	Quatro	*Kwahtroo*
Five	Cinco	*Seengkoo*
Six	Seis	*Saysh*
Seven	Sete	*Set*
Eight	Oito	*Oytoo*
Nine	Nove	*Nov*
Ten	Dez	*Desh*
Twenty	Vinte	*Veengt*
Fifty	Cinquenta	*Seengkwayngta*
One hundred	Cem	*Sayng*
SIGNS & NOTICES		
Airport	Aeroporto	*Aehrohportoo*
Smoking/ No smoking	Fumadores/ Não fumadores	*Foomadohrsh/ Nown-foomadohrsh*
Toilets	Lavabos	*Lavahboosh*
Ladies	Senhoras	*Sinyohrash*
Gentlemen	Homens	*Omayngsh*